The Marshall Chronicles

Farm-to-Market Edition

Capturing Moments
in a
Pastor's Journey

Randy Marshall

The Marshall Chronicles: Farm-to-Market Edition
Capturing Moments in a Pastor's Journey

Randy Marshall

Published by Austin Brothers Publishing, Fort Worth, Texas
www.abpbooks.com

Copyright 2023 by Randy Marshall

The copyright supports and encourages the right to free expression. The purpose is to encourage writers and artists to continue producing work that enriches our culture.

Scanning, uploading, and distribution of this book without permission by the publisher is theft of the author's intellectual property. To obtain permission to use material from the book (other than for review purposes) contact terry@abpbooks.com.

ISBN: 979-8-9867751-3-5

Printed in the United States of America
2023 -- First Edition

Acknowledgments

*"For this reason I remind you to stir afresh
the gift of God which is in you..."*
2 Timothy 1:6

Space cannot fill all those who have helped kindle and stir the fire of God within me, allowing me to spend years in civilian and military ministry.

Allow me to say a word of thanks to a few:

- My mother, who modeled and taught, by word and action, the love of God.
- My dad, who taught me the value of hard work.
- My sister, Sandy, who has prayed and encouraged me all these years. She is a model of inspiration and faith.
- My wife, Susie, who has sacrificially been my "helpmeet" as we have shared life together. Her saying, "Yes, let's go!" allowed us to explore beyond our comfort zone.
- Our children, Blake and Amanda, who have allowed me the privilege to be their dad. They didn't always have the opportunity to say "yes" to the journey, but they were troopers throughout – then and now.

- Our Daughter-In-Law, Lindsey, who has provided love and support to our family.
- Our Grandchildren, Matthew, Emery, and Bennett. They are precious gifts.

Spiritual leaders and friends from Jr. High, High School, College, Seminary, Military, Churches, and Communities we have lived and served. Special thanks to my home church at Kirby Baptist Church in San Antonio. The long-time pastor Ken Brown allowed me opportunities to preach while still in High School. The congregation patiently (and probably painfully) listened and encouraged an extremely nervous young minister in training!

A great thanks to all who prayed, encouraged, and mentored me in my life's journey, stirring afresh the gift of God that was fanned into a glowing flame, enabling me in a small way to shine in my corner of the world!

Contents

Preface	1
Introduction	3

Yorktown, TX

The Journey Begins	9
The Family	13
What Were They Thinking?	15
Dairy Queen & Coffee	19
Chute Leadership	23
Worship	27
More Worship	31
Sweeter than Honey	35
Fine	39
The Touch	43
Community	47
Visibility	51
Blessings	55
The Bulletin	59
Baptism	63
Firsts	65
Another Funeral First	69
Look Who's Watching	71
Transition	73

Stockdale, TX

A New Beginning	77
Be Yourself	79
Everyday People	81
Worship	83
The Sermon	85
Preaching Truth Through Personality	89
Distractions	91
More Distractions	93
Nursing Home Ministry	95
Post Office	99
Getting There	101
How Many More Miles?	103
Royal Ambassadors	105
RA Camp	107
Running to the Store	109
Funeral Home Directors	111
Here Kitty, Kitty	113
Hide and Seek	117
The Intruder	119
Pray For Peace	123
The Association	125
Funny Things Happen at Funeral Homes	127
My First Wife	129
Friday Night Miracle	131
Goose 911	135
Out of Chicken	139
New Doors!	141

Watermelon Jubilee	143
A Farewell	145

Dickinson, TX

Another New Beginning	151
Home	153
Living Water Works	155
PR	157
Amazing Grace	159
National Events	161
Turning 40	165
People Like George	167
Face-to-Face with the Right Stuff	171
Seasoned Adults	177
It's Not Always As It Seems	181
Post Office Encounter	183
On Mission	187
Pets	191
Aren't You My Neighbor?	195
Looking for Randy Marshall	197
24-Hour Silent Retreat	199
Jingling of the Keys	201
Influence	205
The Message	207
Farewell	209
Epilogue	211

Preface

"Sometimes you will never know the value of a moment until it becomes a memory."
Dr. Seuss

Years ago, our family took a trip to *Disneyworld*. My wife and I, along with our two young children, loaded our *Ford* minivan and trekked eastward across Texas, continuing through Louisiana, Mississippi, Alabama, and Florida, eventually arriving in Orlando at the *Magic Kingdom*. Along with our luggage, safely tucked away behind the seats, was a borrowed video camera (yes, a video camera - it was a long time ago!) I used that camera to capture the sights and sounds of the *Disneyworld* adventure. After a few days, we returned home. Upon our arrival, I still had some tape left in my video camera, so I used about ten minutes to record my two young children excitedly getting settled back home, running around, acting silly, etc.

Decades have passed since that trip. The video-tape has long been converted to a DVD. When I occasionally pop the DVD into a player, I find myself impatiently watching footage of the Disney characters, the rides, the shows, the sights, the sounds. I want to yell at my thirty-year-old self, "Turn the camera around!" I don't care about Disney; I want to see my kids! My favorite portion of that old video is the last ten minutes. I have discovered that the most precious family moments were (and are) the everyday moments.

Dr. Seuss was right; sometimes, you will never know the value of a moment until it becomes a memory. Every day has moments to embrace. Scripture reminds us of this, including the Psalmist, who wrote, "Teach us to number our days, that we may apply our hearts to wisdom" (Psalm 90:12). During the hustle and bustle of the day, let us all take time to embrace the moment. Wise living will help us see the unique value of each moment…including moments that eventually become precious and priceless memories.

Introduction

In many ways, I was destined to be a minister:

- I was born in a town named for an apostle – St. Paul, MN
- My mother's name was Betty, short for Elizabeth – the name of the mother of John the Baptist
- My blood type matches my overall demeanor – B Positive
- I have lived most of my life in God's country – Texas

My calling to ministry was confirmed in 1976 while attending a youth ministry retreat at Alto Frio Baptist Encampment in Leaky, TX. I was sixteen years old. Though I cannot fully put the experience into words, it was an undeniable calling of God in my life to serve as a vocational minister. Though I did not know the path ahead, I was eager and anxious to see what God had in store.

Forty-plus years later, I look back at the twists and turns of theological training and practical experience as a youth minister, pastor, and Reserve Air Force chaplain. We all have a story. The book in your hands is my story – a chronicle of selected snapshots of my life, family, and church. This book focuses on the first 22 years of my journey as a local-church pastor. These are real-life events. They reflect experiences of being a pastor, husband, and father that still "stick" in my mind. Some are reflective. Some are insightful. Most are somewhat humorous – which is my preferred take on life (remember, B Positive!).

The journey will traverse the farm-to-market roads of south and southeast Texas, highlighting three distinct churches and communities I had the privilege to serve as pastor – First Baptist Church of Yorktown, First Baptist Church of Stockdale, and First Baptist Church of Dickinson. Though these churches and communities may be "off the beaten path," much activity and ministry occur.

My desire in writing this book is threefold (Baptist ministers always think in threes.)

First, I hope this provides a glimpse into the life of one pastor and family that brings insight, perspective, and a smile to some pastors who minister in their unique churches and communities. Though the context of ministry is in small-town Texas, my guess is, for many, the stories will resonate with those serving in communities of all sizes and geographical locations. Also, though my background is Baptist, men and women from all traditions can readily identify with internal struggles and joys while ministering to a congregation.

Second, I hope this chronicle of one man's journey can allow church members to value their ministers' heart and mind while appreciating their spirituality and humanity. It may be a shock to some that pastors are human too! They have good days and bad days. They face the same physical, mental, emotional, social, and financial pressures as everyone else – sometimes more. Perhaps some of these stories can help gain insight and understanding.

Third, I hope the reader reflects on their own stories. All believers are ministers. Whether the context is at work, home, or play, the Christian has stories to tell! Reflecting on personal life experiences can bring meaning and significance and perhaps even elicit a smile on a distant memory. Reflecting, writing, and telling our unique stories will strengthen, encourage, and revitalize the Body of Christ.

The Marshall Chronicles

So, welcome to the first book of a trilogy of one pastor's life – "The Marshall Chronicles: Farm to Market Edition!"

Yorktown, TX

1986

The Journey Begins

My journey into the pastorate began as a freshly graduated 25-year-old seminarian traveling down I-35 from Dallas to Yorktown, TX. The rented U-Haul and the ten-year-old car following behind me contained all my earthly possessions, as well as my wife, Susie; 10-month-old son, Blake, and daughter, Amanda, still in the womb.

I was in the lead, driving the U-Haul, with Blake in his car seat, on the passenger side (BTW, parents, I know now that it was not safe for my 10-month-old son to be sitting – face forward – in the cab of a U-Haul. It was 1986, and we didn't know any better – At least I had him in a car seat!).

As we traveled the five-hour trip, the scenery slowly changed. We left the hustle and bustle of Dallas down I-35 past Waco, Austin, and various other roadside towns. Turning west off the Interstate at Seguin, we began traveling on Farm-to- Market Road (FM)121. Farm-to-Market roads, also called ranch-to-market roads, were originally built to connect rural or agricultural areas to market towns. Texas established this system in 1949 to improve access to rural areas. Today, the system accounts for over half the mileage in the Texas Department of Transportation system. Communities and churches beside these Farm-to-Market roads are where I cut my teeth in pastoral ministry. As we traveled, not only did the width of the roads change, but so did the topography outside my windshield – more open space – farmland, ranchland, and homes sprinkled among a mesquite-laden countryside.

After several more turns, we found ourselves on the outskirts of Yorktown, in DeWitt County in South Texas. The town was founded by Captain John York and Charles Eckhardt and named in honor of York, a famous Indian fighter from 1835. The population of Yorktown was around 2,000, with a large population of German and Polish residents.

As I drove through the town with youthful exuberance and expectation, I was also intrigued by the quaint shops and well-kept Main Street. My mind projected the great things that were to come. A church had "called" me to be their pastor and entrusted me to be their shepherd – what an honor! I also envisioned what I was going to be able to do for these people who lived off the Farm-to-Market.

I have never considered myself a "city boy," but I am also not a "country boy." If anything, at least at this point, I would call myself a "suburb boy." My Jr. High and High school years were spent living on the outskirts of San Antonio. The church I attended, Kirby Baptist Church, had a small but vibrant congregation with Godly pastoral leadership. This caring congregation and youth ministry led me to attend Howard Payne University in Brownwood, TX, a school known for producing solid ministers. I then attended the largest Seminary in the world, Southwestern Baptist Theological Seminary in Fort Worth, TX.

Let's face it; I had a Texas Baptist pedigree with mountain-top experiences. I could now convey the wisdom from on high to these common, ordinary country people. I kept my spiritual humility in check, of course. Still, I looked at little Blake starting to doze in his car seat and thought, "I'm going to show these people in DeWitt County what "ministry is all about!" The youthful overconfidence and "sitting higher than usual" Uhaul perspective had gotten the best of me. It was not until I could come down from my high perch to the ground below that I could see clearly.

In the days, months, and years ahead, I learned that effective ministry with the church is serving alongside one another. I learned that not only was I investing in their lives, but they were also investing in mine. My journey was their journey. I may have been called "pastor," but these people and congregations I was privileged to serve in the next 22 years would teach me and strengthen my understanding of family and faith lived through the crucible of daily life.

The journey had begun. There was still much to learn coming down from the perch.

Randy Marshall

The Family

The first order of business was to unpack the U-Haul. With the help of eager church members, our furniture was placed, boxes were unpacked, and the church-owned "parsonage" became our home.

Susie and I quickly realized that the gulf between college/seminary life and local church pastorate life was quite a chasm. I don't remember any classes that dealt with this phenomenon. An unexpected challenge was adjusting to my newfound role. In this small community, except for my wife, I was no longer called "Randy." I was referred to as "Bro. Randy," "Bro. Marshall," or "Preacher." Susie was no longer just my young wife; she was the pastor's wife.

Though she was called Susie, she expressly forbid me to call her "Sister Sue!" And, of course, the children were the pastor's children. No matter where we went, we were always the pastor and his family. My opinions no longer became my own, but in this predominately German community where Baptists were a distinct minority, my opinions were seen as those of the church. In turn, Susie's opinions were reflective of the pastor's opinions. The clothes we wore, the language we used, the places we went, the vacations we took, the friends we made, the movies we saw, the food we ate, etc., were all under scrutiny. During these early days of ministry, we both struggled to feel comfortable as a pastor, married couple, and parents.

Randy Marshall

Throughout history, ministry couples have experienced both the joys and frustrations of managing expectations. The stress can be especially weighty on the minister's wife. It has been said that there are two types of pastors' wives. The first type is the woman who has always dreamed of being a minister's wife. She envisions co-laboring with her minister husband in the work of the Lord. She often volunteers for special opportunities like leading the women's ministry or the summer Vacation Bible School. She may play the piano or sing in the choir. She is actively involved in the life and ministry of the church.

The second type of pastor's wife simply loves the man who happens to be a minister. Don't get me wrong; it is not that she is less spiritual or focused than the first. But, unlike the first, her marriage to a minister was not predetermined. A wise minister will identify which type of woman he married and not try to make her the other. Susie is the second of the two types of minister's wife in our home.

Susie and I met during our freshman year at Howard Payne. We began dating my junior year and got married after graduation. She didn't come to Howard Payne to marry a minister. The thought of being a minister's wife somewhat terrified her. Though she falls into the second category of a minister's wife, her loving heart and infectious attitude draw many to her. She loves her husband, she loves her children, she loves her church, and she loves her Lord.

What Were They Thinking?

So, here I was, a pastor of a real church. I knew it was true; it said so, right on the door of my office – in bold letters, "PASTOR." Once I had firmly dismounted the high perch of my U-Haul, ground-level feelings of insecurities and inadequacies began to infiltrate my mind. You see, the concept of being a pastor is much less daunting than actually being a pastor. With boxes of books needing unpacked and placed on the shelf, I sat in my little office and asked myself, "What were they thinking?" "Why are these people entrusting their church to an unpolished 25-year-old newly graduated seminarian?" "How do I even get started?"

Considering the weight of pastoral responsibility, my mind wandered back to an experience at Howard Payne. During my sophomore year, I worked part-time at a local bank. My title was unofficially a "Go-for" – as in "go for this, go for that." My responsibilities included making coffee, straightening the storeroom, receiving/sorting the mail, etc.

One day, a bank official instructed me to go to the post office and pick up a delivery. I drove to the post office, entered my usual place at the rear delivery entrance, and informed the postal clerk that I was there to pick up a particular item that had just arrived. Though I had seen the man several times before, on this trip, he squinted a bit, strangely looked me up and down, leaned forward a bit, and asked, "Do you have a weapon?"

I uncomfortably answered a weak "no." He asked me if anyone was with me that could provide protection. Again, the answer was "no." Shaking his head in disbelief, he went to a back room and came out with an off-white, locked cloth bag. He passed it over the desk to me and said, "Be careful, son, this bag contains one-hundred thousand dollars!"

My eyes widened as I took the bag and wondered, "Why would they give this to me? What were they thinking?" I am certain that security measures have improved over the years. Surely, the post office no longer entrusts locked white bank bags containing substantial money to a 19-year-old college kid who shows up at the back door.

Regardless, I firmly gripped the bag, walked out the door, and scanned the street for any unsavory characters, i.e., shadowy figures in black sedans, strangers at the corner smoking cigars, and anyone wearing a black hood over their face. Seeing none, I walked to my 15-year-old Ford Vega, threw the bag in the back seat, and quickly drove the 3-minute drive back to the bank. I parked the car, looked around again, and delivered the goods to the bank official. She took the bag and said, "Thanks," as if I had just given her a cup of coffee. With the successful delivery, I once again asked myself, "What were they thinking?"

So, back to my cluttered office, I pondered the ministry ahead. This new pastoral responsibility was as if I was once more given an unexpected bag of riches – it was both thrilling and terrifying. The receiving, holding, and delivering of the treasure this time wasn't a quick trip. I was entrusted to this new "Pastor" role for the next few weeks, months, and years. Along with the keys to my new office, this imperfect minister had been given the keys to share a timeless, perfect, God-inspired treasure-filled message on a continual and ongoing basis to a church and community.

I took comfort in the words of the Apostle Paul in 2 Corinthians 4:5-7, who said, "For what we preach is not ourselves, but Jesus Christ as Lord, and ourselves as your servants for Jesus' sake. For God, who said, 'Let light shine out of darkness,' made his light shine in our hearts to give us the light of the knowledge of God's glory displayed in the face of Christ. But we have this treasure in jars of clay to show that this all-surpassing power is from God and not from us."

It is true; the light of God's glory is contained in you and me – jars of clay. The majestic and miraculous story of redemption – the story that has spanned the universe, the story that has changed and transformed lives, the story that will be proclaimed until the end of time – is entrusted to be shared by the church as God's messenger to the world. This light shines not only in our words but also in our lives. This method of eternal redemptive transmission is how God set it up – ordinary people sharing an extraordinary message. But, really, Lord, in this small town led by someone like me – Lord, "What were You thinking?"

In the same vein, my mind then wandered to the birth of our son, Blake. He was so small and vulnerable. Again, though I knew the concept of "dad," the weight of being and daily living "dad" became overwhelming after his birth. I was enthralled to look at him through the nursery window and then be able to hold him with the watchful eye of Susie and the nursing staff.

One day, the nurses told us that we could take him home. So much care was being given to him I forgot we could take him home – by ourselves – no nurses, no counselors, no real instructions. Take him home? I looked at Susie and asked, "Are they crazy? They trust us to take him home?" Susie assured me that she knew what she was doing and that we would be fine. I was a fast learner and began a crash course on being a dad.

Over the years, I found that pastoring is a lot like parenting. We receive instructions, but we frequently wing it – if we are fortunate, we can find our way with a little help from our family, friends, and church community. So, the pastoral journey begins – full of excitement and uncertainty with the still-lingering question, "What were they thinking?"

It would take some time before I was able to embrace my role. Even now, it is humbling to think that the purposes of God are furthered by the imperfect church led by imperfect ministers like me. As I returned to unpacking and shelving my books, I considered God's presence to lead me on this uncertain and (for me) uncharted path. I also held to the words of Paul, who reminded me that "this all-surpassing power is from God and not from (me!) O.K. Lord, You have brought me this far – here we go!

Dairy Queen & Coffee

The First Baptist Church Yorktown church office was located in a building that was built, I believe, when John York founded the city. The long WWII-era building, in need of repair, was situated just behind the sanctuary – divided by a gravel drive. In Yorktown, I was the church staff. The church office wasn't much, but it contained a bookshelf, my desk, an electric typewriter – everything I needed to create powerful, life-changing sermons – at least, that was my hope!

Any leader will tell you that knowing your context or the people you serve in their unique environment is important. Wise pastors will take time to study and "exegete" the community they serve just as much as the Biblical text. Some of the learning will come naturally as a part of everyday life. Other learning takes place serendipitously in unexpected places. For example, though I didn't have it written on my daily planner (as if I needed one), almost every day, around 9:30 a.m., I would hear a pickup turn onto the gravel road outside my office door, followed by a quick two-honk horn. I'd leave my chair, come around the desk, open the door that led outside, and hear, "Hey, pastor, do you want to get a cup of coffee?" Sometimes it was Leo, sometimes Leonard, sometimes Joe, whoever got there first. I'd come around, open the door, and hop in to take a quick drive to the local Dairy Queen.

Once we arrived, the day's driver would buy my coffee, which came in a little red cup with "DQ" on the side. Once there, the two of us usually met up with a group of men much older than me. We would talk. Actually, they talked, and I mostly listened. These men were farmers, ranchers, oil field workers, and retirees. Unlike the seminarians back in Ft. Worth, that would sit around the table and talk theology – the great themes of sanctification, justification, eschatology, and epistemology – these men had a much earthier conversation. They talked about the weather, I mean really talked about it as if their livelihoods depended on it – which it did.

They discussed the local high school football team, "the Wildcats," and dissected the coach's decision at the game last Friday night. They talked about the good old days and how things used to be. Their language would be seasoned with an occasional expletive. Most times, they would say, "Sorry preacher" (as if I had never heard such a thing!). After about two refills from the nice lady from behind the counter who would carry her coffee pot over to her regulars, my ride and I would get up, get back in the truck, and I would be dropped off back at the church building.

So, it was day, after day, after day. Early on, when I heard the horn honk again, I would sigh, "I'll never be able to finish this sermon, but they see my car out there, so they know I'm inside."

I began to sit in the Dairy Queen with my cup of coffee, warming my hand and zoning out of another weather conversation – too wet, dry, cold, hot, etc. My mind would go to a place, and my inner voice said, "What are you doing here? This is what four years of college and three and a half years of seminary got you? These people don't need a pastor; they need a meteorologist!"

But somewhere along the way, God gave me a fresh vision. I don't remember how or the vehicle He used, but the Spirit of God spoke to me! It wasn't a burning bush experience out in the wilderness. God used the glow of the fluorescent lights burning in a small-town restaurant to illuminate me.

The Marshall Chronicles

In my 25-year-old mind, I thought that true ministry was studying, preparing, and presenting the truth of God's Word to a group of people. I was prepared to give a lifelong study of the Biblical text, but God showed me that I also needed a lifelong study of the hearers of the text. I wasn't called to share my life and preach His Word to some people. I was called to share my life and preach His Word, at least at this time, with these unique people in DeWitt County.

I realized I would never be able to touch their hearts if I didn't understand and embrace their lives. A funny thing happened along the way – I was having fun with these men. Their laughter and friendly jabs with one another were infectious. The mornings when I didn't hear the horn honk outside of my door became disappointing – when no one came by on a particular day if I could scrape up 50 cents, I would drive down to the Dairy Queen myself!

All my years of ministry have involved a cup of coffee. I have had conversations with believers and non-believers with a cup of coffee in my hands from Dairy Queen, the local diner, coffee houses, in homes, backyards, front yards, in the church Fellowship Hall, at wedding receptions, after funeral services, at football games, on Mission Trips, during Wednesday Night Bible Studies, at church picnics, playing dominoes, in golf carts, at military dining facilities and just about every place that you could imagine. I have had a lifetime of drinking coffee with family, friends, and strangers – I am much richer (pardon the pun) for it.

My initial Dairy Queen ministry got me out of my comfort zone of examining the text and lunged me into a world where people lived their daily lives. I was able to enter their world, they became more familiar with mine, and our lives grew together – not just as pastor and parishioner but as friends – friends I will always cherish.

Chute Leadership

Honk, Honk!

Up I jump for my coffee break of the day. Inside the somewhat used truck is Big Joe. Joe is in his mid-seventies. His size is as big as his voice. With his closely trimmed flat-top, he looks and has been confused with the former beloved coach of the old Houston Oilers – Bum Phillips. "Morning, Preacher! I'm glad you wore your jeans; I've got a job for you today! (I quickly learned that wearing blue jeans during the week was not only accepted but preferred.) I drank my coffee that morning, wondering what Joe had in mind. The empty cattle trailer being pulled by his truck gave me a pretty good idea.

After three cups of coffee and hearing a lot of bull, we actually went to see a bull and about 15 cows waiting in a cattle pen. I found that cows have a talent for waiting. They wait to be fed, they wait to birth calves, and they wait to be slaughtered. Look into the eyes of a cow, and you will see deadness as if they know what is ahead.

Setting the scene, the cows and bull were in a holding pen. The pen was connected to a chute that forced the cows to walk in single file, leading them to the trailer connected to the truck. Joe looked at me and said, "Preacher, we're going to get these cattle into the trailer."

Instantly, I was focused on the goal. My heart began to beat a bit quicker. These animals were huge, and I was going to be their master! The theme from "Rocky" began playing in my mind. I rolled up my sleeves. I wished that I had a bandana to tie around my head. I was ready for action. (Did I mention that I was a suburban boy?) Joe handed me a long stick. I gripped it tightly and gave the cows a steely-eyed stare. I whispered with a Clint Eastwood swagger through tight lips – "Just tell me what to do!"

Joe explained that he would enter the pen and gently move the cows toward the chute where I would be standing. My sole duty was to stand at the appointed location. A bit disappointed, I asked, "That's it?"

He assured me that cows were skittish and just my presence would cause them to keep moving. Sure enough, the cows slowly lumbered from the pen through the chute where at times, I would say, "Go on."

One by one, they eventually ended up in the trailer. Objective one achieved – cows were secure! Now, for the very large bull.

The bull was a bit more obstinate. When Joe finally led him to the chute, the escape route behind him was closed, and the bull became, well, bullish. He just stopped as if he knew his future in the trailer would not turn out well.

Now by my side, Joe says, "Preacher, you need to whack him to get him through the chute."

Not wanting to hurt the poor animal and knowing that the cows simply needed a little nudging, I took my stick, lightly slapped what would become someone's rump roast, and said, "come on, get in" or something like that. Becoming somewhat impatient, Joe said, "no, you've got to whack him!" He grabs the stick and swings a swing that would make any major league baseball player proud. He really whacked him! The bull jumped slightly and moved through the chute and into the trailer. Objective two complete. For my part, at least, mission accomplished!

Over the years, I thought a lot about that day and the lesson of leadership (of course, the analogy breaks down when you consider that I was leading animals to the slaughter – but stay with me!) As you know, cows are much different than sheep. Cows are herded, sheep are led. Perhaps that is why Jesus calls himself the Good Shepherd and not the Good Cowboy! A study of Scripture will show that He led men and women to the truth through his words and actions. He never twisted the arms of unbelievers; he shared and invited others to follow. His presence was enough to draw others to the truth. Scripture is also full of examples, especially in his interaction with the Pharisees, Sadducees, and other religious leaders, where a firmer approach was necessary. At times, he even spoke very directly to his disciples.

As the shepherd to the flock that God has entrusted me, this young pastor was reminded that I am called to follow Jesus' leadership lesson vividly illustrated that day by the chute. Most people need a quiet word, a gentle reminder, a spoken truth, or a hand on the shoulder to redirect them into the path that glorifies the Father. Others who are a bit more bullish need a stronger hand and a firmer voice to move forward.

I think that all pastors tend to rely on one style over the other. We have all seen pastors at the extremes – those too soft, those too hard – both have negative outcomes. Handling difficult people takes a lot of prayer, discernment, and counsel from others who have gone down this path. Listen to those in discord, understand them, encourage them, pray for them but, if need be, admonish them to protect the rest of the flock. Most of all, lean on the Good Shepherd and be reminded of the Psalmist who said, "...even though I walk through the valley of the shadow of death, I will fear no evil because You are with me, Your rod and your staff, they comfort me..."

In prayer, bring your sheep, cows, and bulls to Him, and He will direct your path and guide your hand.

Worship

Ministry in Yorktown wasn't just drinking coffee and herding cattle. Pastoral ministry involved visitation, counseling, business meetings, committee meetings, and community involvement. It encompassed special events like weddings and funerals. As a small-town pastor, I was also the counselor at summer Youth Camps and Children's Camps. I drove the church van to associational meetings, youth trips, and special outings. God Bless the pastor of smaller churches!

The Sunday Morning Worship Service was at the core of the week. This is by far the most visible activity of the pastor and the church. It was here that I would mingle with my flock before Sunday School (holding a cup of coffee in a Styrofoam cup.) After the classes began, I was left alone in my office for 30 minutes to review the notes I had prepared throughout the week. This was the culminating preparation in what had been a weeklong endeavor.

Immediately after preaching my second sermon of the day on Sunday night, I would begin thinking about the following Sunday morning sermon. Ideally, I would have identified a Biblical text to deliver the following Sunday's sermon by Monday. I often preached from one book of the Bible at a time, so the next text was the next Scripture.

Once identified, I tried to do what pastors describe as "live with the text" - truly immerse myself in its meaning and create an outline in my mind. This has always been the hardest but most rewarding part of sermon preparation. By Friday, I would have grasped the text, found pertinent illustrations, and hopefully developed a powerful application. Saturday would be spent with my wife, Susie, and young children. I would review the message on Saturday evening, go to bed early, and wake up to a new Sunday.

This was the ideal. I like the idea of the ideal; unfortunately, it rarely happened so easily. Sometimes, the problem was early in the week. Like a bad-fitting suit, for whatever reason, I didn't feel comfortable about the development from "what the Bible says" to "how this applies to the lives of the congregation." It's hard for people to grasp, but pastors are actually human. They fight the same spiritual, mental, emotional, and physical battles as everybody else. In the quietness of the study, they think about who they should be visiting, why they haven't seen so-and-so lately, how they are going to live on a small church salary, what the next church program should entail, and why no one has come by to buy me a cup of coffee!

Their emotions can be all over the place – sadness, anger, greed, jealousy, the whole spectrum – but the gamut of emotions was always kept in check because, well, they are the pastor! Physically, most pastors would say they need to be more active, but the church, family, and social schedule seems too demanding. It's also frustrating when you have a great message planned and wake up on Sunday morning with a scratchy throat and a hacking cough! All this plays into the pastor's mind as he sits in his office preparing a sermon for Sunday.

You may have noticed that Sundays come fairly regularly –about once every seven days! Don't get me wrong; the process was exhilarating most weeks as I could move from words on a page to seeing a light come on when the Word of God came alive.

Susie and I discovered early on, that Saturday night was "discuss nothing heavy night." Before we made that rule, we would inevitably get into some discussion that led to an argument that raised my blood pressure and put a cloud on my Saturday night sermon "dry run." Let me tell you; it is hard preaching on the love of Christ when you have had a run-in with your wife!

So, on Sunday morning, I sit in my office, notes firmly placed in my Bible, ready to go. Early in my ministry, I wished for a pneumatic tube – the kind the banks use for outside tellers – to shoot me from my office straight to a spot directly in back of the pulpit at the given time to deliver the message. Inevitably, before I could filter these kinds of things, the short distance between the office and my place on the stage was fraught with distraction. People would want "to speak a word with you." "The word' was frequently negative or at best trivial. The air conditioner wasn't working in the nursery, someone said something sharply toward someone else, some dear soul wanted to tell me about her exciting vacation – with pictures, someone had a gripe about something. Most of these things deserved the pastor's attention, but did it have to be immediately before I preached?

Hopefully, despite the preacher's frailties and the congregation's idiosyncrasies, the Word of God was prayerfully prepared and powerfully proclaimed!

More Worship

Worship will embody men and women, young people, boys and girls, focusing on praising the Lord, hearing his teachings, and responding to His calling. This is worship in the purest form. The songs we sing, "Holy, Holy, Holy," "Blessed Be the Name of the Lord," and "Lord, I Lift Your Name on High," remind us that we are mere mortals and the only hope we have is far beyond ourselves, that we can only exist because of an omnipresent, omnipotent, omniscient, and everlasting God. Those big words I learned in seminary basically mean worship is all about Him.

Though that is certainly true, worship also involves us. One of the mysteries of the church and Christianity is that God chooses to involve us at all. Going back to worship in the synagogue, then the Temple, the church of the past, and the church of today, we tend to muddy the waters.

The purity of worship becomes somewhat polluted by our preferences, opinions, biases, and a thousand other human contributions. A hallmark of Protestants is the centrality of God's Word. God's Word is central to our teaching, preaching, and beliefs. Walking into a church, you often see the pulpit in the center of the stage. Though some Christian denominations will hold to a Bible plus Church Tradition stance, Baptists staunchly hold to the Bible alone as their source of authority. Don't be fooled, though; Baptists also have spoken and unspoken traditions, especially among churches near the Farm-to-Market. Woe to the minister who messes with some of these long-held sacred cow traditions.

For example, many can remember, and perhaps your rural church has one today—a scoreboard located prominently in the front of the sanctuary. The wooden board gives statistical information on attendance and offering. Normally, it provides the Sunday School offering given on that Sunday compared to a year ago. It also provides today's attendance with attendance from a year ago. O.K., no one calls it a scoreboard, but it provides the worshipper a sense of progress or lack thereof.

I admit when I made my way into the sanctuary from my study; I would look at the board. If the offering/attendance was trending up, I felt satisfied. If it was trending down, I was a bit discouraged. If the numbers were down, then I must be doing something wrong. Maybe it was just the congregation. Maybe it's the community. Why are there so many Germans in this town? The Lutheran and Catholic services are booming!

Admittedly, this is not a good way to prepare for a worship service. Again, the purity of worship is to focus on God; the humanity in me was to focus on me. Let's face it; it is extremely difficult to measure spirituality and success. One of the challenges of ministry is the inability to have a finishing point. There is always a sermon to prepare, a visit to be made, and a prayer to be prayed. The personal and professional work of the minister is ongoing.

Even when the scoreboard shows upward trends, it is still an artificial metric. More money and more attendance are important when we talk with our fellow pastors, especially when they ask the commonplace question, "So, what are you running these days?"

This translates to: "How healthy is your church?" and "are you an effective leader?" Though the board may measure numbers and noses, it is a small indicator of what is taking place in the church. True spiritual markers such as growing disciples, caring for those in need, and lives touched by the power of the Gospel are not normally annotated on a wooden board. As a young idealistic pastor, I questioned the purpose of the scoreboard but was never brave enough to suggest taking it down.

Music is another area of high sensitivity and tradition. Musical form and style have been debated since the early days of the church. The early Christian church had very simple tunes based on the tune and meters of songs popular in the day. Accepted church music has run the gamut, from simple tunes to the Gregorian chant to songs, hymns, and choruses. Common instruments today, such as the piano and organ, were once suspect because of their association with the secular world.

First Baptist Church, Yorktown, worshipped with hymns, normally sang from the hymnal. One of the advantages of hymns is the connectedness to the past. The old hymns remind the worshipper of religious and spiritual experiences of long ago. In the '80s, praise choruses were introduced in churches and were met with varied responses. For many, they did not seem to fit the form and style of a First Baptist Church.

Occasionally, the volunteer music leader would attempt to teach the congregation a new chorus. Instead of using the hymnal, the words would be printed on a piece of paper. Being progressive-minded, I suggested we print the words on transparency paper and put the words on a screen projected by our overhead projector. This would save paper and make the words more visible. Sounds good, right? I was quickly informed that this practice is what charismatics do in their worship! Next thing you know, we will be raising our hands! I laugh now because it is common today to walk into Baptist churches of all sizes to see a mounted video projector displaying not only words but graphics.

Looking back, it is also a reminder that 1) Some changes are before their time, maturation still needs to occur, and 2) Changes in a rural church come slowly. I heard a saying years ago: "Don't confuse your theology with your methodology." Our theology should always be rock solid; there should never be a drift from the fundamentals. Our methodology should and must change.

The methods we utilize must be current. When we confuse the two, then conflicts come. Another distinction I have learned is the difference between tradition and traditionalism. Tradition is defined as the "living faith of the dead." Traditionalism is "the dead faith of the living." All of us can laugh at things we used to hold firm and now seem so archaic. May we always keep a firm grip on our faith (theology) and a loose grip on how we express our faith (methodology.) May we also allow the richness of our traditions to illuminate our present and future endeavors in the kingdom of God.

Sweeter than Honey

As a young minister, I underestimated the importance of the choice of Biblical translation used in preaching and teaching. Following the lead of professors at Howard Payne, I came to Yorktown using the New American Standard Bible (NASB.) The NASB, so I have been told, is one of the most literally translated modern Bibles staying true to the original Hebrew, Aramaic, and Greek languages. I have also been told it is a reliable, scholarly translation for serious Bible study.

What I soon learned, however, is that the NASB was not a favorite or even known translation in Yorktown. Though it is a literal translation, it can be a bit choppy in the English language. I learned that the two predominant translations used in the church were the King James Version (KJV) and the New International Version (NIV.) The KJV, also known as the "Authorized Version," originated in 1611. Though for some, the language is archaic and obsolete, many appreciate its dignity and majesty. The NIV was published to provide a modern translation by Bible scholars. For many, the translation helps the reader understand and clarify the Old English language of the KJV. The NIV is currently the most popular translation today.

In reality, each translation tells of God's redemptive work. Though some truths are expressed slightly differently, the truth remains. So, in light of this fact and the New International Version's popularity, I switched to the NIV. I actually have many translations of the Scriptures in my possession. I still have my NASV, a couple of NIVs, a New Testament Bible that contains 24 different translations, two foreign translations, a "Good News for Modern Man paraphrase, a small KJV that was given to me as a child, a large KJV suitable for the coffee table and a KJV Thompson Chain Reference Study Bible.

My KJV Thompson Chain Reference Study Bible is unique. You could even say it is one of a kind. No matter what translation, most Bibles begin with the book of Genesis – the book of beginnings. However, if you open the cover of my 40-year-old, black, King James Thompson Chain Reference Bible, the top of the tattered first page says "Leviticus 11."

No, I didn't buy this Bible at a steeply discounted bookstore. No, I didn't have a theological meltdown and decide to eliminate the stories of creation, the patriarchs, the exodus, and other foundational truths of the Old Testament. I have a justifiable reason for owning an incomplete copy of the Scriptures. I have an excuse. It is one of the oldest excuses known to man – the dog ate it! Really.

One spring day, I decided to review my sermon on the back patio at my house, accompanied by my dog, Licky. Blake named the dog Licky because he (the dog) liked to lick. Regardless, I left my KJV Thompson Chain Reference Study Bible on the backyard patio table for just a moment. A few minutes later, I looked out my window with a glass of sweet tea in my hand. Much to my surprise and chagrin, I saw my dog – hind legs on the chair, front legs on the table, wet nose in the Bible – devouring chunks of sacred history! How was I to know he preferred the King James! By the time I sprinted outside, he had already systematically partaken of Genesis, Exodus, and a portion of Leviticus.

With the ragged, dripping Bible safely in hand, I stared at him in disbelief. He looked at me with a typical canine cock-of-the-head silent response, like, "What? What did I do?"

I looked up into the cloudless sky and was grateful for the absence of storm clouds. Surely, one of us would be struck by lightning by defacing God's Word! After my holy anger had subsided, we eventually made our way back inside. BTW, as a trained theologian, I carefully observed his behavior over the next several days. Partaking of rich, historical truths did not seem to affect his personality. He still barked at the neighbors, dug holes in the yard, and acted like a dog.

If he had chewed a little further, he would have come to Psalm 119:103, "How sweet are Your words to my taste! Yes, sweeter than honey in my mouth!" This knowledge could have caused him to stop and bark out an enthusiastic "Amen!"

Actually, the imagery of feasting on God's Word is a frequent theme throughout the Old and New Testaments. The call of Scripture is to heartily partake of the Word, meditate upon it, and digest it, enabling the penetrating message to permeate and nourish our lives.

Though, I would not encourage anyone to physically chew on pages of Scripture, maybe my old dog was on to something. Perhaps if more people had the same excitement and focused energy on devouring and ingesting the truth of God's Word rather than constantly debating and defending it, we would find ourselves closer to the God of the Bible. Though dogs cannot rise above their four-legged nature, God has infused us with the capacity to know and experience Him. The truth of His Word can transform us, both inside and out, today and for eternity.

So, through a lifetime of discovery, I have found that whether you read or listen to your Bible on the printed page, personal computer, laptop, tablet, or smartphone, we should be willing to dig in with joyful expectancy. Whether we prefer a modern translation or the majestic Old English language, we can regularly, and with great expectation, take a bite of God's Word in various sizes and chunks. We can then savor its sweetness and allow the taste of truth to melt in our mouths, fill our souls, warm our hearts, and renew our minds! I can now say,

Randy Marshall

"Thanks, Licky!" Your strange, unexpected behavior has become a real eye-opener!

Fine

One of the unspoken traditions of many smaller churches is the expectation that the pastor will greet the parishioners as they exit the sanctuary following the closing song. Stealthily, during the final stanza, I would move from my position at the front of the sanctuary around the side aisle to my position just inside the entrance door. When the song ends, women gather their purses, kids, and husbands and greet me as they exit. I admit, to the outsider, it is a rather odd tradition. After all, I have already talked to most people before Sunday School, after Sunday School, and right before worship. But I stand at the door to wish them well.

Adults and kids with parents come by and wait patiently to exit through the front door. Youth normally make their way to one of the side exits. Standing at the back also provides an opportunity to receive instant feedback. Since most people are not bold enough to insult the pastor on his preaching style – they wait until they are in the car – most give a polite nod and smile. Sometimes a comment is expressed, such as, "Thanks for that sermon. I really needed to hear that" (my personal favorite).

"Thanks for keeping the sermon short; you know the Cowboys play at noon."

"According to my Bible notes, you preached from that same passage two years ago."

"I heard (insert favorite radio preacher here) preach from that text last week – it was really good."

"The sound system was messed up again today."

"Why don't you use the King James Version?"

"You are getting better every week!" A well-intentioned comment to a young preacher, but what I heard was, "You're not there yet, but you are better than you used to be!"

As people passed, I would give some standard statement such as "It's so good to see you today," or "Have a great day," or some personal comment about the week that I was familiar with, like "Joey sure had a great game on Friday night didn't he?" or "I'll be praying for you about..."

One of my basic out-the-door questions would be, "How are you doing today?" The standard answer over three pastorates was "fine." Though that person's family life may border on intolerable, relationships may seem irreparable, and financial pressures may appear insurmountable, they smile and say, "Fine."

It's an easy answer. They look around, and everybody else at church appears to be fine. Everybody seems to be happy and holy. It's hard to be the only one not living the good life. Somehow admitting to the pastor at the door that life is less than desirable, especially when he just preached a sermon on abundant life, can seem sinful.

In our high-paced, success-driven world, we feel that we must keep up the façade to hide the truth. On the surface, this seems like a practical solution to our pain. The problem with this approach, of course, is that we never move past the surface. This avoidance attitude can even affect how we relate to our God. Surely God expects us to be happy. He doesn't want to hear about our aches and pains, does He? Actually, what God desires is for us to be real. When we are real before Him, laying out our hurts, pains, and disappointments, He is willing and fully able to provide direction, wisdom, and power. When we are vulnerable before Him, He moves past the façade of fine, below the superficial surface, and directly to the heart of the problem.

I must admit, in Yorktown, there was one precious senior adult I learned never to ask, "How are you doing?" because she would stand at the door without awareness of the growing line behind her and tell me. She would tell me about her numerous aches and pains on top of her troubles, trials, and worries. As she went on, I would have my best concerned, pastoral face on, trying to stay focused on what she was saying. I quit asking her because I didn't want to hear all her woes. I quit asking because asking produced a response. The response took time, and I had other hands to shake.

My attitude reflected the attitude of those around me. We can get so focused on the waiting crowd and not give attention to the hurting one. Come to think about it, perhaps if we took less time to shake hands and more time to truly listen, people would get the idea that it's O.K. to move beyond "fine."

The Touch

A Pastor must learn the fine art of touch. One of my Dairy Queen lessons was the value of a firm handshake for respect and survival! A pastor's hands are generally less calloused and worn than a rancher's or farmer's. Most men understand this and will give you a pass when they shake hands, though they will notice. What they do expect, however, is a manly, firm grip when exchanging greetings – especially if you find yourself in rural Texas. Woe to the individual who gives a weak handshake.

Nothing can erase your "around the Dairy Queen table credibility" faster than a weak handshake. Shaking hands with some can also be a test in itself. You can identify this person by how he twists his mouth, maybe adjusting his chew, squints his eyes, and puts out his right paw like a gunslinger in the old west. Just a word of wisdom from experience, when he pulls his hand out of the holster – seize the moment! Don't hesitate; immediately put your hand in his hand and make sure that the space between your thumb and forefinger is squarely in the same space in his hand. Otherwise, even if you are a bit short of that spot, he will take your hand and put a vise grip on it that will suck the blood from even the smallest capillary.

This is a planned move. He will be smiling a devilish smile because he knows he has you in his grip. If you find yourself at the Dairy Queen in this situation, keep shaking, smiling, and resisting the urge to cry like a baby because the blood is now depleted from your hand, and bones are beginning to crush. Keep the hold until the ten count. He will eventually let go because a manly shake has a time limit.

Afterward, if need be, drink your coffee from your left hand to hide any discomfort. Also, never discuss the matter unless you write a book about these things. Especially don't tell your wife. Her reaction will be 1) Laugh at you and tell you that you're a bit wimpy, or 2) she would actually know this grip guy, and she would say something to him. The secondary effects of this are much worse than the original infraction.

Conversely, like a professional football player coming home to his wife and infant daughter, the pastor must also know that one of the top ten worse things you can do is crush the hand of one of your senior adult women. So, in the church, especially in the line at the back of the church, the pastor is constantly adjusting the approach and the grip of each congregant depending on their sex, size, age, body type, and profession. It can be an exhausting endeavor until this constant adjustment becomes second nature.

Another move that pastors acquire is the use of the left hand. In non-church settings, the left hand never comes into play. It lays innocently on the side of the shaker, except for the occasional slap on the arm. In church, however, again, especially at the back of the door, and when receiving those during the invitation, the pastor will find himself greeting the individual with the right hand and then slipping his left hand to the left arm or shoulder of the recipient. It is a classic pastoral move. It's not really a hug, but it completes the circle of fellowship.

Touch is an important part of the church, particularly with the elderly widows of the church. Sunday is the only day they have received any touch. A gentle word accompanied by a gentle touch can communicate volumes and endear you to your people. Touch includes hugs, but hugs themselves can be somewhat touchy. You, your wife, and your church context must figure this out.

In my experience, the safest hug was the public hug to one of our senior adult ladies. Normally, as my wife calls it, it was a one-armed hug – somewhere between a two-armed hug and the classic right hand of fellowship and left arm on shoulder. It was simply a warm greeting.

I love to hug children, but sadly in our society, I always ensure other people are around. One somewhat grey area was women my age and under. Some women are just huggers who would hug me spontaneously – one and two-armed! Most of the time, with most women, my wife wouldn't mind this spontaneous hug. But some, I could feel her laser eyes burning into my forehead from across the room. I knew later that we would talk. In the car, on the way home, after a few moments of silence, she would say, "I don't trust _____." My first thought was hyper-spiritual: "We just left church, and you are talking about people you don't trust." What I would say would be, "She's just giving me a hug." She would look at me and say, "You better watch her." This meant, "I am going to watch her!"

Men, your wives have a keen discernment of the emotional side of women. Listen to her. She may not always be right but listen to what she is saying. Surround yourself with people willing to say (and you give permission to share) words of wisdom in this area. Your touch is powerful. It is a gift that communicates compassion and empathy. In our technology-driven, insulated society, touch is a catalyst for a greater spiritual connection. Like most gifts, Satan can also use it to communicate something beyond comfort and pastoral care, even unintentionally. Be aware, but don't be afraid to touch people. Follow the model of Jesus Himself, who was continually touching those he came in contact bringing hope, peace, comfort, and healing. Keep touching; just make sure the touch is open, visible, and above reproach.

Community

A well-worn term in church life is the word "fellowship." Many churches have a large room next to the kitchen called the "Fellowship Hall." This is a place where people gather for special "fellowship lunches and suppers." The events can even be advertised as "Food, Fun, and Fellowship."

"Fellowship" expands beyond this room. On Sunday morning, it is common to greet one another with "a right hand of fellowship." If we want to hang out together during the week, a spiritual way we can express it is, "Hey, why don't we get together and fellowship this week?"

"Fellowship" is defined as a "friendly association, especially with people who share one's interest." This definition can refer to a group of people in various activities. This friendly association can be seen at the local Lion's Club, a Chamber of Commerce meeting, a football game, a stamp collecting club, etc.

Christian fellowship, however, is much deeper. Most Christians would trace their meaning of fellowship to the New Testament Greek word "koinonia." Fellowship is a connection to God and His people. Paul states, "God is faithful, through whom you were called into fellowship with His Son Jesus Christ our Lord" (I Corinthians 1:9). Luke expounds on the connection of this relationship to God with the connectedness of fellow believers. In speaking of the early church, he records, "They were continually devoting themselves to the apostles' teaching and to fellowship, to the breaking of bread and to prayer... and all those who had believed were together and had all things in common" (Acts 2:42, 44).

The early church set the tone for churches of every size and location today. Both in the worship service and everyday life, there is fellowship, also known as connectedness, or very commonly referred to today as community. Though our salvation is very personal, out walk with the Lord is drawn toward community.

Small-town life is very communal. Conversations at the Dairy Queen expand from Friday night football games to discussions at the City Hall to gathering to honor one who has died. In Yorktown, the community had close family ties. These family ties were extensively interconnected.

Growing up in a military family, I did not have a regular connection to my extended family – my immediate family consisted of myself, my older sister, mom, and dad. In Yorktown, it was not uncommon to visit a married couple and discover that their mom, dad, uncle, children, grandchildren, brother, brother-in-law, sister, sister-in-law, nieces, nephews, and other assorted relatives lived in Yorktown or surrounding DeWitt County. I was fascinated and somewhat envious that the family lived so close and community was so strong.

There certainly is an upside to the closeness. People know each other and have a history together. There is also a downside. People know each other and have a history together! The dynamics of small-town life is a case study in itself and would take much more space than this book can contain.

I will say that both positive and negative, there is a depth of relationship in most small towns uncommon in big city life. People know each other. They look out for one another and their children. There are likely teachers in the schools teaching children of children they taught twenty years prior. There is a barber who cuts the hair of family members across generations. These family members and the newcomers, who may have lived in the community for a mere 15 years, gather at various places of worship to experience an even deeper community. At least, as a minister of one of those churches, that is the hope – a need to experience the presence of God with like-minded, spiritually transformed Christian community. Ministry is in a particular context. The wise minister will be cognizant of the uniqueness of the small-town church and the community served.

Visibility

I quickly found that the person in the pew wants to see more than just the pastor in the pulpit. They want to see if the pastor is real. Can he be trusted? Does he believe and live what he says? Is he a man of integrity? Is he a Dallas Cowboys fan – a determination of these and other serious considerations? The best way to reveal and demonstrate these qualities is through regular interaction with the church and community.

Unlike some of my big-city counterparts, the small-town pastor (and family) is always on display. Whether within the confines of the church building, at the local supermarket, at the high school football game, mowing my lawn, or just walking around town, I was seen as "the pastor." I'm sure over the years, people would look at me and proudly say, "That's my pastor!" I'm also sure that there were times when, perhaps not at my best, people would look at me with disappointment and say, weakly, "Yep, that's my pastor," or even worse, "that's my pastor?"

During these days, I often met people in town and heard them say, "You don't look like a pastor." I never knew if that was a great compliment or a veiled insult. I am reminded of the cartoon that shows a man sitting on a park bench and commenting to the older lady sitting next to him, "No, ma'am, I'm not a minister; I've just been sick for a few days." Maybe, when people said, "You don't look like a pastor," they meant I was young and vibrant, I had a great outlook on the future, etc... maybe. Maybe they meant, "You don't look like you have experienced enough life to tell others how they should live." Perhaps the truth was somewhere in between.

Visitation is key to the success of a small-town pastor. One of my first visits was with an older woman who lived alone in her small frame house. I knocked on the door and gave enough time for her to answer. She escorted me to her small living room – big enough for her stuffed chair, couch, and box TV. As we talked, I noticed, right above my head, a wooden frame encompassing the room. I also noticed the frame was connected to a pulley. Knowing that elderly people have all sorts of aids to help them get around, I asked her, "So, does this frame help you get up from your chair?"

She looked at me for a few seconds and then let out a hearty laugh! When she caught her breath, she said, "Boy you sure are green!" Come to find out, that frame was a quilting frame – something this suburbanite had never seen. My inexperienced "greenness" was showing. It was simply another reminder that I still had a lot to learn.

I kept pressing on, attempting to interpret my ministry environment. I would continue to drink my coffee, make my visits, and just show up. I would attend funerals of people I didn't know. Though I didn't know the deceased, several of my church members knew or related to the grieving family. I would sit and grieve with them. I attended football games, band concerts, and various community events. I learned oilfield lingo like "roughneck," "drilling rig," "toolpusher," "driller," "derrick hand," and the purpose of "drilling mud." I learned that the oil company "Schlumberger" is pronounced "Schumberzhay" and the town down the road "Refugio" is pronounced "Referio."

I learned that cattlemen don't think very highly of sheepmen. I learned that "that" family never agreed with anything said by "this" family. I learned that when someone said, "You can't get there from here," you really could. I learned that directions could be tricky. One day, I asked where Mrs Johnson lived. Oh, it's easy, just go down 119 and turn by the old barn. Go a few miles down the caliche (another word I learned) road and take a right when the road Ts. Go a couple of miles until you get to the old tree that was struck by lightning ten years ago; go a little further. She lives in the old Smith home. In this pre-GPS era, I commonly responded, "Can you draw me a map?"

I have always been inquisitive. I want to think that the churches and communities I served appreciated and endured my attempt to acclimate to their world. One of the great truths of Scripture is that God became flesh. He is God incarnate. John 1:14 says, "And the Word became flesh, and dwelt among us, and we saw His glory, glory as of the only begotten from the Father, full of grace and truth."

God "emptied" Himself from the glory of heaven to be born in humble circumstances to show us His will and way intimately. The Gospels tell that He dwelt among us. He walked in our midst. He laughed and cried. He ate and drank. He taught, and He listened. Yes, Jesus listened. He listened to the concerns, perspectives, philosophies, and grumbling of his disciples and those He came in contact with.

I always thought it was interesting that Jesus, in calling His disciples, said to them, "Come, follow Me, and I will make you fishers of men" (Matthew 4:19). Jesus, the then 30-year-old carpenter could have said, "Come, follow Me and I will make you builders of men." Though Jesus does refer to some building imagery throughout his earthly ministry, his initial and primary picture of ministry is a fisherman. Why? Because Jesus was talking to fishermen. He was talking with those accustomed to casting nets into a body of water with the expectation of catching fish. Jesus not only lived with them, but He also spoke their language. Throughout my ministry, I have attempted to emulate the example of Jesus by being present with the people I serve – not only to teach and lead but to listen and learn.

Blessings

As I settled into the pastoral role with coffee, visits, conversations, meetings, worship, and sermons, my immediate family was about to expand from wife and son to wife, son, and daughter. When it became evident (in the middle of the night) that Amanda was fast approaching, Susie and I went into action. We already had a bag packed. We had spoken to a couple who agreed to watch Blake when the time came. So, in the car, a quick stop to drop off Blake, and on the way to Cuero (twenty-minute) drive to the community hospital.

The hospital staff greeted us and later the family doctor (who was a deacon at the First Baptist Church, Cuero). As with Blake, Susie had a long delivery. Also, as with Blake, I was by her side until Amanda's birth. In the '80s, having the father in the delivery room was a fairly new phenomenon. I understand that years ago, dads could sit in the comfort of the waiting room reading fishing and golf magazines while drinking a cup of coffee.

After all the drama behind closed doors, they were then given the news like everybody else "It's a boy," or "It's a girl." I was fortunate to be part of the time to be part of the drama with each excruciating step. It's only fair. Making the baby was a joint venture. I was there in the beginning; it is only right that I was in the final process. It makes it easier to tell people that "we are having a baby."

Randy Marshall

Since I was present at Blake's birth, I knew the drill. I had even been trained in a special "Lamaze" class. I don't know what Lamaze means, but I am guessing it references pain. For the uninformed, the woman in labor is hooked up to a monitor. This monitor measures contractions. Some are small and subtle; some are large and intense. The longer the labor, the more intense the contraction.

My main role in the process was to sit by my wife, hold her hand and watch the monitor. What was interesting (at least to me) was that I could see the blip on the screen indicating a contraction even before Susie felt it. So, as a loving husband, I was able to prepare her and say something like, "Honey, the contraction is coming. I'm here for you." She would smile and hold my hand a bit tighter. It was beautiful. It could have been a Norman Rockwell painting.

After several hours and increasingly stronger contractions, the Rockwell picture lost its luster. Weariness and frustration began to set in – and for Susie as well! At one point, with me at my monitor post, I looked at the large blip on the screen and said, "Wow, this is a really big one!" For some reason, the gratefulness she expressed hours earlier had faded! I decided to press on, nonetheless.

Once she was fully ready, she was whisked to the delivery room with me in tow – dressed in scrubs and a white mask. I discovered with Blake's delivery that I could never be a surgeon. Aside from the lack of mental aptitude and physical ability, the mask would have done me in. For me, inhaling and exhaling through the cloth material was next to impossible. At one particular moment, when Amanda's entrance into the world was moments away, I became faint with beads of sweat coming down my face. At that point, time seemed to stop as both my wife and the doctor stopped and asked, "Are you O.K.?" I assured them that I was fine and that they should carry on!

After the delivery, Amanda was premature and had trouble breathing. With Susie left behind in Cuero, I traveled with Amanda by ambulance to a larger hospital in Victoria, some 30 minutes away. She stayed in ICU for a week while we made daily visits. On Sunday morning, we gathered again for worship. Community once again became an even greater focus. I stood before a loving congregation with full knowledge of my exciting, albeit stressful, week. I don't remember what I preached; however, I do remember one particular hymn we sang, "Because He lives" The first two stanzas are:

> "God sent His Son, they called Him Jesus
> He came to love, heal and forgive
> He lived and died to buy my pardon
> An empty grave is there to prove my Savior lives."

And then....

> "How sweet to hold a newborn baby
> And feel the pride and joy he gives
> But greater still, the calm assurance
> This child can face uncertain days because He lives."

So, I sat on the stage holding back tears. The child that I could not wait to hold was in ICU. It was a bit gut-wrenching. However, I was also able to focus on the calm assurance that this child and our family could face uncertain days because He lives.

And the chorus....

> "Because He lives
> I can face tomorrow
> Because He lives
> All fear is gone
> Because I know He holds the future

And life is worth the living
Just because He lives."

Support, prayers, encouragement, understanding, and all the qualities of a loving fellowship, not only from the church in Yorktown but my home church in Kirby, not to mention family and friends, were overwhelming. It was not the first time I had experienced this level of love and support – and it certainly was not the last.

The Bulletin

Unlike some of my colleagues, I never had to print a bulletin. I have mowed the churchyard, unclogged toilets, unlocked doors and locked doors, power washed, painted the church (both inside and out), picked up cigarette butts, swept the sidewalk, climbed on ladders and roofs to trim trees, changed light bulbs, vacuumed dirty floors, wet-vacked flooded floors, prepared PowerPoint presentations, run the soundboard, attended youth camps, children's camps, mission trips, VBS and done a hundred other things for the church, but I have never had to print a bulletin.

FBC Yorktown did not have a secretary, but the church did have a nice older man – diminutive in size but knowledgeable about the world, 80-something-year-old Mr. Cole. He had provided his volunteer services to prepare the bulletin for years. I knew about bulletins. Growing up at Kirby Baptist Church in San Antonio and then as a youth minister at Buckner Terrace Baptist Church in Dallas, I watched secretaries prepare bulletins. Any minister in the '80s knew bulletins were produced on the mimeograph machine. For the uninformed, a mimeograph machine was designed to make multiple copies from a stencil.

The secretary would put the special waxed mulberry paper stencil in the typewriter, removing the typewriter ribbon so that the bare, sharp letter or symbol struck the stencil directly. The impact of the type element displaced the wax, making the tissue permeable to the oil-based ink. It was called "cutting a stencil."

Once prepared, the stencil was wrapped around the ink-filled drum of the mimeograph rotary machine. When a blank sheet, or the back of a bulletin shell, was drawn between the rotating drum and a pressure roller, ink was forced through the holes on the stencil onto the paper. (For those who have no idea what I just wrote, or wonder why they didn't just use their computer, ask your parent or grandparent to explain!). Though it was laborious by today's standards, it was a pretty good system for its time and had been around for years.

In Yorktown, whatever machine Mr. Cole used, and I assumed it was a mimeograph machine, was located at his residence. He would come by mid-week, and I would give him the hymn numbers and sermon title, which changed from week to week. What didn't change, I noticed, was the format of the service and the weekly schedule on the right side of the bulletin. It was the same, week after week.

Being the innovative young pastor, I decided that we needed to change things up a bit. I began giving Mr. Cole current announcements and upcoming events along with the normal material. I noticed a deer-in-the-headlights look on his face the first week I presented this to him. About the third week, I asked him if he could put a picture or two in. He just turned around, shook his head, and left. In the fourth week, I planned on going by his house anyway, so I would drop off the ever-growing bulletin material.

His "shop" was in the back of his two-story frame house. It was a lone trailer with rickety steps leading to a worn-out door. When I opened the door, I was stunned. I felt as if I had stepped back in time. Whereas a mimeograph machine can easily fit on a small table, Mr. Cole possessed a machine far bigger and much older. The antique machine, the size of a refrigerator, was a moveable type machine.

Moveable-type technology goes back to the year 1080 under the Chinese Song Dynasty. It developed into the printing press, which later fueled the Reformation across Europe. What Mr. Cole possessed was an adaptation of this same technology.

Through a series of pulleys and levers, windlasses, tympans, and friskets, it could make 3,000 copies an hour – far more than what FBC Yorktown required. The time-intensity was in creating the forms. Each individual metal letter punch had to be hand loaded and locked into the form to make the template. I had been working Mr. Cole's fingers to the bone for the past few weeks. This volunteer octogenarian silently suffered under the young pastor's "innovativeness." I quickly apologized and asked him if we could revert to the old way of doing things – just changing the hymn and sermon. He seemed to like that idea.

This was another lesson learned about carefully placing an undue burden on others under the banner of the pastor's vision. It's easy to cast a vision, but we must be willing to put our hands to the work. In other words, ministers need to not only be vision setters but also be willing to empathize with the type setters!

Baptism

As you can imagine, for a "Baptist," baptism is a highly regarded observance or ordinance in the church. As well it should be. Baptism is an outward expression or picture of the new believer's death, burial, and resurrection. For the uninformed, baptism in a Baptist church is by immersion – another way of saying they are dunked.

In most cases, the minister stands in a large tub-like structure with water up to his waist and baptizes the new convert. The structure is called a baptistery. Growing up Baptist, seeing a baptistry was commonplace, but Yorktown's baptistry was unique. The designer of the church and its baptistry was either very judicious in his use of space, or he didn't like ministers.

As in most churches, the baptistry was directly behind the choir loft. Behind the wall of the choir loft, on either side, were restrooms. In Yorktown, the restrooms were "one-seaters" with a sink. In the corner was a makeshift ladder. When it was time for a baptism, one of the deacons would hook the top of the ladder onto the entrance of the baptistery door, some seven feet above the floor. The ladder would then be placed at a 45-degree angle, over the toilet, beside the sink, and slightly past the restroom door. The pastor and the brave new convert would climb the seven feet, where a ledge led to three more steps into the water.

Randy Marshall

One particular Sunday, early in my Yorktown pastorate, I was baptizing a teenager who had a Lutheran background. Her parents were somewhat leery about their Lutheran daughter being immersed, something she insisted. They saw a change in her life and wanted to be supportive. So, they and other family members came to worship at the First Baptist Church on the day of baptism for this teenage girl. I wanted to show the family that Baptists love the Lord as much as Lutherans, and we celebrated the Holiness of God in our own celebratory tradition. So, at the end of the service, I don my waders and ascend the wooden steps with Bible in hand.

At the appropriate time, I descend the three wooden steps down to the floor of the baptistery. When I take the last step, I step a little to my right and hear a snap. Under the water was a two-by-two piece of board that connected the set of stairs on the right side with the set of stairs on the left side. I kept walking toward the center of the baptistry, now facing the congregation. As I reverently read the Scripture, I notice something odd. Because of the broken support, both sets of wooden stairs were slowly rising to the surface of the water. I kept reading.

No one in the congregation could see the wayward stairs. When I finished reading, I placed my Bible on the ledge and gave a pastoral pause. There were two sets of wood floating on the surface and one perplexed young lady looking at me from the side. Finally, I announced that I needed a couple of deacons to assist me – they were confused because we were breaking protocol. They ascertained the situation and then proceeded to clumsily push the stairs back down and hold them until I could baptize the young girl, and we were both able to exit to the top of the stairs. Mission accomplished, but zero style points!

Firsts

Funerals are a sacred time. In all my years of ministry, I never felt more useful than when officiating a funeral. The congregation gathered that day comprises local family members, family members who have traveled a great distance, and friends. Nothing can compare to words spoken by a pastor through the truth of God's Word to the heart of those who are grieving. It is a holy, somber time, but again because it involves people, some funny things happen at a funeral. Funny things happen at finely orchestrated weddings – no matter how much planning takes place.

I conducted my first funeral and first wedding on the same day. That is an irony in itself. I have been a pastor of a "First Baptist Church throughout my ministry." It is not uncommon for funeral home directors to contact local church pastors to conduct a funeral service for individuals who have no church home or preference. If someone comes in and says they are or used to be "Baptist," then I would normally receive a call. From day one, my feeling was that I would do it because of the intense grief, pain, and loss if someone needs a funeral preached, and I am available. Funerals can be pivotal points in people's lives as they come face to face with the frailty of life.

The challenge of conducting my first funeral was that I had only been to two other funerals in my life. I knew people who had died, mostly elderly, but I only attended two funerals for some reason. I attended a fine Baptist college and a prestigious Theological Seminary. Still, surprisingly, I was never taught how to give a funeral message – or for that matter, serve the Lord's Supper. It was one of those "jump in the water; you'll learn to swim" moments! The service went fine. I remembered the deceased's name, and my sermon seemed to make a difference. So far, so good.

Typical of the pastor's life, I quickly changed hats and began thinking of the upcoming wedding. I counseled the couple two times and gave them some homework – which is still my practice today. They were "older," in their mid-forties, the second marriage for both. On the afternoon of the wedding, Susie and I drove to the ceremony site.

The location was not at a church building or a wedding chapel; it was down several country roads in the backyard of the groom's home which opened up to a large open field with cows grazing in the background. The music was coming from a keyboard. The seats were rectangular bales of hay. The groom wore jeans, a country shirt, and a bolo tie. The bride wore a white dress with a country vest. Both wore boots. I wore the suit I had worn earlier at the funeral (my marryin' and buryin' suit).

Weddings are holy moments as well. As the presiding minister at a wedding, I have the best seat in the house. I can see and feel the emotion as the two conveyed their love for one another. Because of the pressures on a marriage, I always pray that it sticks. When I conduct a funeral, people tend to stay buried – that is not always the case when I conduct a marriage!

The ceremony went fine. I again correctly pronounced the names of both the bride and groom. The night was cool and clear; no one fell off any hay bales. The setting sun made a beautiful backdrop. To top it off, when I pronounced the newly married couple as husband and wife, a cow bellowed in the background, right on cue!

Susie and I drove back knowing that in the past 10 hours, we were a part of two significant family events, though the contrast couldn't have been more stark – a somber funeral in a funeral home and a joyful wedding out in the country.

It was a good day to be a pastor in DeWitt County!

Another Funeral First

Funerals can be highly emotional events. In the event of a sudden death, the family can still be in a state of shock, simply going through the motions. Even when the death was long-anticipated, a feeling of finality can be overwhelming. The minister is a sort of guide to assist in dealing with emotions and giving a heavenly viewpoint on life and death. Whether familiar with the deceased or not, I always spent time with the family to gain understanding and insight into their loved one.

On one occasion, I spoke with the family concerning a young man who had died in a motorcycle accident. These family members did not look like the majority of the citizens of Yorktown. They were part of the biker community and had the stereotypical look of long hair, multiple tattoos, and weathered faces.

On the day of the funeral, at the funeral home, the crowd matched the family's look. I was able to speak some words of comfort from the 23rd Psalm, that even as we walk through the valley of the shadow of death, our God is with us. All seemed to go well. At the end of the ceremony, as was the custom, I stood at the head of the open casket as the congregation filed by the body and shook my hand and the hand of the funeral director, who stood to my right. It was at this point that the unexpected happened.

As they were filing by, an argument erupted between two men. Suddenly, out of nowhere, one man pulled and opened a switchblade.

With eyes wide, I froze. Nowhere in my theological education and my wildest dreams was I prepared to know how to respond. Fortunately, the funeral home director, who undoubtedly had seen it all, quickly intervened and diffused the situation.

I will say that this event was never repeated in my years of ministry. It was a wake-up call that anything and everything can happen in ministry. It is part of the great adventure!

Look Who's Watching

A classic example of "you never know who's watching" happened outside the church parsonage on a beautiful sunny day. The church parsonage was located a couple of miles from the church building in an established neighborhood. One day, my wife (yes, the pastor's wife) and I were in our yard, to the side of the driveway, under an Oak tree. We had put a blanket down, and both lay on it, talking about how great life was. Blake was playing nearby, and Amanda was on the blanket in her baby carrier – a normal couple enjoying the moment with their young children.

Later that week, my wife talked to our across-the-street neighbor, who ran a beauty shop out of her garage. Nonchalantly, she said, "I saw you and Bro Randy making love in the front yard last week."

Time stopped. My wife's eyes widened. Apparently, at least in her vernacular, the term "making love" included any affection, even a stolen kiss. From then on, we realized that our actions were very public. I made a point after that only to make love inside!

During this same time, we were trying to teach Blake how to "poopoo" and "peepee" in the potty. He had the #1 down pretty well but had a problem mastering #2. One day, Susie was washing dishes and watching Blake in the driveway riding his Big Wheel. She missed a very important event. Blake came running into the house with tremendous excitement. He grabbed Susie's hand and led her out the garage door to the spot where the love-making took place. There in the grass was a pile of preacher's son poop! He was so excited that he didn't go in his pants, and here was the proof.

Susie was congratulatory but realized that our son needed some additional instruction. As she took Blake's hand to go back inside, she glanced back at the neighbor's house. If she saw anything, she never said, and we never asked!

Transition

In May 1989, I accepted a call to become the pastor of the First Baptist Church of Stockdale. Years later, at the church's 80 anniversary, I wrote these words of thanks and memories.

Friends at First Baptist Church, Yorktown,

Congratulations on your 80th anniversary! Though Susie and I are not able to attend the celebration, you are held dearly in our thoughts and prayers. I had the opportunity to serve as your pastor from 1986-1989. You took this twenty-five-year-old, recent seminary graduate into your trust to preach, teach, pastor, and provide spiritual leadership to your families and community.

You were part of a series of monumental moments in our lives – introduction and appreciation for small-town life, the birth of our daughter, the beginning of preschool for our son, and my ministerial ordination. You were an integral part of a series of personal ministerial firsts – first pastorate, the first officiant of a wedding, first funeral, first Lord's Supper, and first Baptism.

While drinking many gallons of coffee in the old fellowship hall, around kitchen tables, and down at the Dairy Queen, I learned about your dreams, desires, and disappointments. Through Worship Services, Bible Studies, VBS, children's camps, youth camps, Gambrell Baptist Association meetings, and countless other gatherings, you al-

Randy Marshall

lowed me to enter and speak to your spiritual lives. As a young pastor, husband, and father, you taught me a lot about life and real ministry. I have carried these foundational lessons throughout my 29 years of ministry, both as a pastor and military chaplain.

Thank you for your care and influence that has had a long-lasting impact on my life and family. Thank you for your dedication to ministry – to the children, youth, and adults in Yorktown, DeWitt County, and across the world. Though we are not there to give you a physical hug, we embrace great memories and shared experiences with a loving congregation. We hope you have a great day of celebration as you take a reflective look to the past while anticipating the great things that God has in store in the days to come.

God's rich blessings upon you all,
Randy, Susie, Blake, and Amanda

Stockdale, TX
1989

A New Beginning

After three productive years at First Baptist Church, Yorktown, the Lord called us to First Baptist Church, Stockdale, just 30 minutes away.

The phrase "the Lord called us" is somewhat foreign to the uninformed. Baptists have a different system, unlike some denominations that regularly move ministers from one location to another. Since Baptist churches are local and autonomous, the calling of a minister rests with the local congregation. There is no ecclesiastical authority that influences or directs local church actions. As Baptists like to say, the "Baptist Headquarters" is located at the local church.

At the right time, there is a connection between a church looking for a pastor and a pastor open to a move. There are obviously several human factors involved. It is the prayer and hope of all that God is working amid the process. It is not a perfect system, but in my opinion is best of all, giving the Spirit of God space and freedom to work.

So, in 1986, the Marshalls arrived in Stockdale. The First Baptist Church is located squarely in the center of Stockdale, Tx.

Stockdale is located at the crossroads of Hwy 87 and Hwy 123 near County Roads 401 and 414. Previously, the area was named High Prairie, Free Timber, and Bunker's Store. Stockdale was named after Fletcher Stockdale, the lieutenant governor of Texas when the town was established in 1863.

Though the population of Stockdale was fewer than Yorktown, the church was a bit larger, and the makeup of the church was a bit more diverse. The town was still rural. The church included school teachers, administrators, carpenters, a banker, employees who worked in nearby San Antonio and Seguin, homemakers, restaurant workers, and of course, some ranchers and retirees.

It was a new environment, but with three years of pastoral experience under my belt, I was ready for a new challenge.

Be Yourself

We loved Yorktown. We made some good friends. I will forever be indebted to a group of people who took the chance to call a freshly graduated seminarian to be their pastor. Their confidence in my ability and willingness to follow my leadership was amazing. But Susie and I both endured growing pains in acclimating to our new environment and being comfortable in our ministry role. At times there was a certain "stiffness" as we attempted to conform to what we thought a minister and wife should be.

When we moved to Stockdale, we both saw a need to change our approach to ministry. The change was simply to be ourselves. We were happier, the church was responsive, and Stockdale quickly became home.

Speaking of home, our new home was once again a parsonage. This time, it wasn't down the street. It was directly adjacent to the church building – literally, next to the church. The church building and the parsonage were just a few feet away. At first, I was not thrilled with this. I had heard stories of church members of other churches who considered the parsonage their home and how they would regularly drop in. This was never the case for Stockdale. Our home was a sanctuary for our family, and my morning commute was just a few steps away.

Let the new journey begin!

Everyday People

Similar to Yorktown, Stockdale was full of everyday people. They didn't put on big city airs and weren't trying to impress their neighbors. It was a tight-knit community that took care of each other. If someone got sick, someone would bring chicken soup. If there was a death in the family, out came the casseroles. If a house caught on fire, the local volunteer fire department would respond, and later folks would pitch in to assist in the rebuilding. Though the glory days of downtown Stockdale were well in the past (at least in the '80s), the community spirit was alive and well.

It was not uncommon to come home and find a grocery bag full of fresh vegetables from somebody's garden on our back porch door handle. We often had no idea who gave them, but we were always grateful. One of our members, Burt, would mow our yard and trim our bushes. He would also scratch his head, wondering how a patch of grass was worn in a particular 8-foot by 3-foot area. Yes, the kids' slip and slide caused some damage, but they had fun!

Whereas the pace of life is quick and demanding in the city, most days, the pace in these rural communities is slow and deliberate. Most people were not in a hurry. This was both a comfort and a challenge for me.

In my youthful exuberance, I saw areas of the church that needed attention. I soon discovered that introducing any change, no matter how small, took time to absorb and digest. Taking a lesson I learned from Yorktown, just having the title "Pastor" doesn't mean you are instantly their pastor. Trust is built over time. Pastoral competence must be observed while Pastoral character is being evaluated. There are sermons to preach, Bible Studies to be led, visits to make, funerals to conduct, weddings to officiate, and a thousand other opportunities – publicly and privately to display my worth.

"Is he also a genuine everyday person like us?" Only time will tell.

Worship

Yes, we continue to worship! Each Sunday provided an opportunity for the people of God to gather, sing praises, and hear a message from God's Word. One major difference between FBC Yorktown and FBC Stockdale was the music program. Stockdale was fortunate to have a part-time Music Minister, Howard Hudiburg, a music professor at a university in San Marcus. This enabled the church to have a professional touch and a creative atmosphere.

A major creative step for this country church was an elaborate outdoor Easter presentation. Utilizing an artist in the congregation, a series of professional backdrops were created and placed on a flatbed trailer. Complete with costumes and willing church participants, the church hosted a multi-day presentation of the death, burial, and resurrection of our Lord. It truly was a gift to the community.

Previous to the elaborate outdoor presentation, the church hosted a scaled-down, yet just as powerful, event to focus on the true meaning of Easter. A key character in both the indoor and outdoor presentations was the individual who portrayed Jesus. He was gifted in this portrayal bringing realism to the suffering of our Lord.

One Sunday afternoon, before one of the practices, he stood on a platform that held the cross. He was in character, going through the motions, mentally preparing himself. It was a busy day, and several items had to be addressed. I had not yet spoken with him, and as I hurriedly passed by, I looked up and casually asked, "How are you doing?"

Whether intentionally or not, He spoke to me in a voice that Jesus would use and asked me, "How are you doing?" I instantly stopped in my tracks and weakly responded, "Good."

To me, the picture could not have been clearer. Here I was, a man of the cloth, casually walking by "Jesus," who was on the cross. I hurriedly walked by and flippantly asked how he was doing. He spoke to my soul by asking me the same question. As we capture moments, let us always be aware of moments when Jesus captures us. Let us never be in such a hurry that we miss what God has for us – especially when it comes to the ordinary and routine.

Though our weekly Worship is regular, let it never be ordinary and routine.

The Sermon

What would a worship service be without preaching? Realize that is a rhetorical question! Though every good Christian expects a sermon on Sunday morning, there are a lot of opinions on what a good sermon entails. Some would say an effective sermon includes a gripping illustration, a powerful conclusion, and putting the two as close together as possible!

I have found that people want a powerful word from God, one that captures the original meaning of the passage and provides a modern-day application. Two things should ideally happen to accomplish this: 1) the preacher prepares and communicates effectively, and 2) the hearer practices active listening. The preacher can only influence half of this equation!

Those who come to listen must navigate a myriad of obstacles. These obstacles include prior history of churchgoing, attitudes toward preaching/worship in general, connectedness and confidence in the preacher (does he know what he's talking about), spiritual receptivity, and the ability to sit still for 20-30 minutes. Add other factors like having an argument with a spouse, getting the kids dressed, wondering about the clanking sound in the car, finding a parking spot, and then discovering someone has the audacity to sit in your pew!

To top it all off, unlike most forms of communication, verbal communication is one-sided. The preacher gets to do all the talking. This reminds me of the little boy who told his mom that he wanted to be a preacher when he grew up. The mom, bursting with pride at their son's desire to serve the Lord, asked, "Why do you want to be a preacher?"

The boy replied dryly, "The way I figure if I have to be in church my whole life, I might as well be the one talking!"

Another obstacle for the listener is just being tired. Sitting still this long is an opportunity for some to zone out and maybe close their eyes. Studies have shown that if you took all the people who have fallen asleep in church and placed them end to end, they would be much more comfortable!

I have found theological narcolepsy to be a real condition! For some, deep truths lead to deep sleep. One of my regular members in Stockdale told the story of a conversation he had with a previous minister. The pastor approached him after the worship service and said, "I saw that you were sleeping during my sermon."

The man replied, "That's true, but if you noticed, I was awake when you started!"

I believe the man told me this story to preempt any conversation I may have with him.

Preachers of all generations have been encouraged by the story of Eutychus and Paul. In Acts 20:7-12 we read of Paul preaching a long sermon. A young man named Eutychus (his name means "lucky") had positioned himself on a window during the meeting. The New International Version records, "Seated in a window was a young man named Eutychus, who was sinking into a deep sleep as Paul talked on and on."

As Paul talked on and on, a man named Lucky not only fell asleep, he fell from the third-story window to the ground. It appears that the man died from the fall. Paul stops his sermon, throws himself on the young man, and puts his arms around him. 'Don't be alarmed,' he said, 'he's alive!'" (Acts 20:10)

Yes, even in the midst of greatness, sleep can be overwhelming. This is comforting. The way I look at it, people don't sleep in front of people they don't trust. For some listeners, I am a very trusted person!

Preaching Truth Through Personality

There are many positive statements about preaching. Many of these come from pulpit giants. One phrase I have embraced was spoken by the 19th Century preacher Phillips Brooks. In his lectures on preaching at Yale University in 1877, he said that preaching has two essential elements, truth and personality. It is primarily a testimony to faith. He said preaching has to be face-to-face, person-to-person, and heart-to-heart.

Preaching is not about the preacher; however, the preacher's personality should shine through. In many ways, preaching exposes the preacher. It exposes his faith and theology. Through it, our God-given personality shines through.

The truth, Phillips Brooks said, "must come through the person, not merely over his lips, not merely into his understanding and out through his pen....It must come through his *character*, his *affections*, his whole intellectual and *moral being*. It must come genuinely *through* him. Therefore, preaching must reflect not only our identity but our integrity and our authenticity." (Preaching Truth through Personality – Through a glass, darkly (through-a-glass-darkly.com)

I have discovered two things about my personality that are evident in my preaching. First, I am naturally inquisitive; I always have been. I like to ask questions. I like to place myself in the Biblical story and wonder what it was like. It is exciting to me to dig deep and grasp the theological truth. Once grasped, I also like to envision the hearers of the sermon. Where are they coming from, their struggles, how does this word affect them, etc.

Asking questions is also part of my leadership style and asking things like, "How does this fit in our mission," "What is the purpose," "Is there a better way?" Those who have been around me very long are not surprised by this!

Second, I enjoy humor. I am not a comedian and do not tell stories just to get a laugh, but humor is both enjoyable and powerful. A well-told and well-timed humorous story can open windows of understanding, even while preaching the most difficult topic or intense moment. It is not only a great tool for preaching, but it also carries us through rough stretches.

Early on, in my youth minister days, a pastor said to me, "Randy, take what you do seriously, but don't take yourself too seriously." It is O.K. to laugh at the situation or ourselves. It is O.K. to be self-effacing. Humor must also be guarded. What pops into our minds may be inappropriate or ill-advised. If in doubt, don't!

Personality is powerful. In a somewhat scary (probably unofficial) study, it was noted that after three years, the church begins to take the on personality of the pastor. Take that for what it's worth!

Distractions

Going back to the story of Paul and Eutychus, the reader should note that Paul doesn't allow a man falling to his death stop him from his talk/sermon. The passage says that Paul returned upstairs, ate a snack, and talked until daylight.

Distractions are part of proclaiming God's Word. I preached my first sermon as a teenager. I was surprised at what the preacher could see from a raised platform. After that, my back row behavior improved dramatically. In something only preachers and maybe speakers, in general, can understand, when preaching a sermon, it is on a sort of mental split-screen.

On the one hand, the preacher is focused on the words coming out of his mouth. They are a product of the notes before him, backed up with hours of preparation with an intent to communicate effectively. At the same time is another mental screen. Usually, it runs in the background as the words are coming out. The subconscious is rolling out random facts like, "I think the mike needs to be turned up; I'm not even sure if it's on." Or, "It is warm in here; I hope I don't start coughing." Or, "I'm preaching on love, and my wife is glaring at me!" Incredibly, the sermon continues even through constant subconscious interruptions!

Sometimes the interruptions are more visible. Babies cry. Doors slam. The sound system squeals. A phone rings. A phone keeps ringing. A phone rings, an audible voice asks if everything is alright, and the hard-hearing senior adult recipient answers. (O.K., this didn't happen in the '90s, but it did eventually happen!) One Sunday (in Stockdale), a man toward the front of the congregation began to clip his fingernails during my sermon. Clip, clip, clip, clip, clip could be heard as it echoed in the sanctuary. Though I didn't look, judging by how long it took, he must have also removed his shoes and started on his toenails!

In Stockdale, for the majority of my pastorate there, we had theater seats from the 1950s. They were uncomfortable, which was bad for those suffering from theological narcolepsy. A couple of times, a small child would stand on the seat. If they stood too close to the back of the seat, it would collapse, and the child would be caught in its vice. This would immediately cause a bloodcurdling scream. The damage would not be severe, but it would require a couple of men to release the child. These are moments that cause the pastor to stop. But, like Paul, the sermon must go on. No harm, no foul, no blood – let's move on!

More Distractions

Sometimes the distractions hit close to home. As mentioned, the parsonage was next door to the church building. Our children wanted another dog. The church leadership was gracious enough to have a chain-link fence built. We were given a little dog. The dog was cute, but its bark was extremely annoying. It was one of those barks that seemed to go on and on like the repetitive sound of clicking fingernails.

One Sunday, we left the dog outside, in the fence, next to the church, and he barked incessantly. The second mental screen was beginning to overtake the first screen. All I could think about was the barking and the distraction for me and the congregants. I believe the church leadership was beginning to question the wisdom of buying a fence.

A second memory of a distraction close to home was on a Sunday when Susie was helping in the church nursery. Small-church pastors know the drill – since we didn't have paid nursery workers, there was a sign-up of those willing to help. It was Susie's turn. That left 8-year-old Blake and 6-year-old Amanda sitting by themselves in the congregation. In order to have them close, I had them sit on the second row.

They were generally well-behaved until the sermon. Amanda had pulled her sweater over her head and then pulled it back down for some reason. When she did, the static electricity in her long hair made it stand straight up. She could hear a few giggles behind her. So she did it again with the same result. Though she knew she had become a distraction, she enjoyed the attention, and really what could Dad do about it?

To her surprise, I stopped the sermon and said, "Amanda, go back to the nursery and tell your mom what you are doing."

With wide eyes and a wry smile, she trotted off to the back. She didn't know that there was a speaker in the nursery, and Mom heard what I said. Susie told her, "I don't know what you did, but if Dad had to call you down, it's not good."

Immediately after the service, when I was at the back door shaking hands, she did what she often did and stood by my side – with my arm around her. What she also didn't know at that moment is though she was loved, she would have a stern conversation with her dad later on!

Distractions of all kinds are part of the church experience. Like all moments, they should be embraced!

Nursing Home Ministry

Some of my church members were residents at the local Stockdale Nursing Home. Nursing Homes can be forgotten places in our society. They contain residents facing their last days – sometimes those days extend into weeks and years. Most would say they are beyond their years of productivity; however, I have found individuals in these facilities who teach some important life principles. Qualities such as:

1. Value of Community
Some, but not all, residents knew each other before they arrived. This is one of the positives of small-town life. Though nurses and assistants are readily available, these men and women take time to care for one another. If someone is sad, a loving arm is extended. If someone drops an item, assistance is given to pick it up. When it is time to eat, they gather together.

2. Love of Laughter
These residents love to laugh. They like to tell jokes. They like to kid each other.

3. Examples of Perseverance
Not every resident is aware of their condition. Those who are aware know that this place is not ideal. They would rather be in their

own home, their family member's home, or even assisted living. But, most are also realistic in knowing this is where they need to be.

4. Importance of Worship

Stockdale churches would take turns providing a Tuesday afternoon "worship service" in the community room at the Nursing Home. At the appointed time, residents would gather independently or be wheeled in by an attendant. These services would not only include Baptists but all who loved the Lord and wanted to sing songs and hear a word from the Lord. I would lead a couple of songs and then give a short devotion. Two memories of these services stand out.

First, in the middle of one of our worship services, one of the dear ladies said I was cute. Her wheelchair-bound friend said, "Shame on you; he is married and has children!"

Her reply to me was, "Do you have a brother?"

Yes, even in the nursing home, residents were still full of life – and questions!

Second, one Tuesday preceding the weekly service, I really did not want to go. I was tired. I didn't want to expend the energy, but I did. I begrudgingly arrived and shortly started leading an old hymn. Some of the residents were already asleep or seemingly non-responsive, some were looking at me but not singing any words; some were singing the best they could. My thought on this day was, "Is this really worth it? Does it make any difference?"

Understand, these thoughts were going through my mind as I was leading the music with a smile on my face. In the middle of this internal conversation, I noticed something. Directly to my right was a precious saint singing at the top of her weakened voice with a broad smile on her face and the obvious joy of the Lord in her heart. Her life was being touched at this moment. Similar to the florescent revelation at the Yorktown Dairy Queen years prior, God revealed that He loved these people. They, in turn, loved Him. True worship was taking place. The Spirit of God was at work, and I almost missed it.

Like many religious gatherings, food was also involved. After the service, we would dismiss to the dining area to have some punch and cookies. I would often walk a few steps down the hall to see a young man in his thirties. Years prior, as a boy, he had suffered a bicycle accident that had left him in a vegetative state. I could come and sit by him. To my knowledge, he did not know I was there. He had no way to communicate. His eyes were open, but they were blank with no comprehension. I would quietly talk to him, hoping he could sense my presence. I would also say a prayer for him and his family.

Though some would say that residents at a Nursing Home are past days of productivity, the local nursing home taught me otherwise. Though I would go to give them something, many times, I left receiving emotional and spiritual gifts that touched my soul. This included my visits with the young man down the hall who helped slow my steps, center me, and give me time to reflect upon the blessings of my life and family. Just his presence taught me more than he would ever know.

Post Office

For much of my life, if I wanted to mail a letter, I would walk to the end of my driveway to a little black box with a rounded top and place my letter in it. It was also the place I received my mail. This was a normal occurrence.

In Yorktown and Stockdale, to get and receive mail, I would get in my car and drive to a building with dozens of little gold-colored boxes, all in a small confined area from about knee-height to shoulder height. With three turns of a combination, I would receive my mail. These were called Post Office boxes (P.O. boxes); of course, the building was the Post Office.

In the days that I used to go to the mailbox at the end of the driveway, it was fairly uneventful. Occasionally, I would wave at a neighbor as I thumbed through my mail. The trip to the Post Office was a uniquely different experience. First, I had to ensure that I was properly dressed because, well, you know, I'm the pastor! Secondly, I had to make sure I allotted plenty of time. Woe to the small-town pastor who doesn't stop and talk to people at the Post Office.

Since this mail depot was a major hub for the people of Stockdale, it was one of the busiest places in town (O.K., busy for Stockdale, at least!). It was not only a repository of letters and packages, but it was also a social gathering location. People would stand outside the door talking to friends they hadn't seen since yesterday.

Upon greeting these small groups, I would enter the glass doors of the Post Office, which immediately put me in the middle of the small room containing the P.O. boxes. After greeting a few more folks, I would make my way to my box and, after three turns, open the box and get my mail. Most days that was the extent of the excitement.

Sometimes, however, the box would contain a green card indicating I had a package. That was a thrill, except it meant going through another glass door to wait in line and talk to some more people. Finally, I would come to the counter and exchange my little green card for a big package – at least one bigger than my 2x3 inch P.O. Box. Then, I would make my way to the exit, back through the doors, greet people I didn't see when I came in, make more small talk and greeting to those still gathered outside, and finally, into my car. That's the small-town postal experience.

Looking back, one of the great attributes of having a P.O. box was rubbing shoulders with the community. Like Forrest Gump and his box of chocolates, you never knew what you were going to get or what you were going to hear, or who you were going to bump into at the Post Office.

Whether you were the School Superintendent or the School Janitor, the local Bank President or a waitress at the local café, all in-town residents came by the Post Office, came to their designated box, turned their three turns of the combination, twisted the knob, opened the box, and retrieved their mail. Each of them rubbed shoulders with the other for at least a few minutes every day. In a very subtle way, it helped build a sense of community. It makes you feel sorry for those who only make it to the end of the driveway.

Getting There

"Dad, where are we?"

The little voice I heard was from my daughter, Amanda, then five years of age. She had been looking out the window for the past 10 minutes being relatively quiet and still, which for her, was unusual. When she was a baby, long before she learned to talk, she was in her car seat (in the back seat, of course!), just jabbering away. It didn't matter who was listening; she was talking.

When she learned the English language, she would constantly ask questions about everything. Why is that man smoking? Where is that little boy's mother? How do you make Ice Cream? Why does it rain? When do we get to go home? Why are caterpillars green?...you get the idea.

So the fact that she was quiet was unique. Finally, after some obvious contemplation, she asked, "Dad, where are we?"

So, I replied, "We're on our way to San Antonio."

She frowned, "No, I mean, where are we?"

I was a bit more descriptive, "We are on our way from Stockdale to San Antonio, just past Sutherland Springs."

Still not satisfied, "but, exactly, where are we?"

I said, "O.K., we are on Hwy 87, currently midway between Sutherland Springs and LaVernia at mile marker 45 on our way to San Antonio."

I would have given her the GPS coordinates if I had them, but that was about as descriptive as I could provide.

She finally slumped down in her seat, crossed her arms, and stared forward with a disgusted look – "You don't know where we are." More silence.

I let the silence hang – some things just have no answer.

How Many More Miles?

Another question raised by my children was, "Dad, how many more miles?"

On any long car trip, it was an inevitable backseat inquiry. Blake or Amanda would lean forward and ask, "Dad, how many more miles?"

Sometimes the question came hours into the trip, sometimes before we even left the driveway! I would grin because when I was a kid, I asked the same thing. There is something innate in all of us, wanting to know what's ahead, what to expect, and when we will arrive.

I would often relate the story of my children asking, "how many more miles?" at funeral graveside services while looking at John 14:1-6. Jesus, in comforting the disciples, said, "Let not your hearts be troubled, you believe in God, believe also in Me. In my Father's house are many mansions, if it were not so I would have told you. I am going there to prepare a place for you. And if I go and prepare a place for you, I will come again and take you to be with me so that where I am you will be also. You know the way to the place I am going."

It is here that Thomas, one of the disciples, inquires, "Lord, we don't know where you are going, how can we know the way? Jesus answered, "I am the way, the truth and the life. No one comes to the Father except through Me."

Thomas, perhaps on his back seat perch, wanted more information. He wanted to know the way. He wanted to know, "How many more miles?" The answer for him and us is to listen to Jesus, who says, "Trust me." You want to know the way? Jesus says, "Follow me; I am the way!"

On our journey, there are uncertainties. Some days will bring surprises, both good and bad. Some days may bring heartache or heartbreak. New days bring hope and promise, but the lurking shadows ahead also produce anxiety and uncertainty. We may find ourselves, even as adults, whispering an inquiry in the ear of our Father, "Lord, how many more miles?"

This may translate, "Lord, how many more years do I have on this earth?" or "How can my life make a difference along the way?" or "How long do I endure this sickness, pain, relationship?" or "can I have a crystal ball to see what the future holds?"

Our heavenly Father, in His wisdom and mercy, doesn't reveal the details of the future. He doesn't give us a GPS or a phone app to map our quest. While He provides the tools of Scripture and Prayer, He gives Himself the most important gift. He is both Holy and approachable; He is "Immanuel," "God with us."

As believers, when we whisper into the ear of the Lord, we can be assured He understands our questions, fears, and misgivings. We can also be confident He has a firm grip on the wheel and will navigate us through bright sunny days, as well as through the thickest fog and the darkest night.

As we journey by faith in His presence, we know that our God will personally and intimately lead us on our path. He will guide us through life's twists and turns, heights and depths, ups and downs. To top it all off, as believers, we know that when this life is in our rear-view mirror, He will triumphantly lead us home – that's where one journey ends and another glorious one begins!

That is a message for children, those in grief, and for each of us today as we journey through life.

Royal Ambassadors

Stockdale had a Royal Ambassador program. Royal Ambassadors (RAs) was a program for elementary-age young boys to gather and learn about Jesus. Think of it as a church-centric Boy Scout Program. The girls had a similar program called "Girls in Action" (GAs)

The RAs program in Stockdale was multi-faceted. First, they had a weekly after-school program. Each Wednesday, the children would come to the Fellowship Hall, where they would be provided cookies and sugary drinks. They would then be led in an activity, and a Bible story would be told. Again, this occurred after a long school day and stomachs full of sweet cookies and sugary drinks! Looking back, I am not sure how much learning actually took place!

Another aspect of the RA program was taking an annual overnight campout on some property a few miles out of town. Children would be loaded up and carried about 10 miles to a barren land sprinkled with Mesquite trees. Adults, like the pastor, would accompany the children. Once at the location, we would prepare the camps by setting up our tents, starting a fire, and listening to the rules. One important rule was that a hole would be dug where all would relieve themselves when needed. This was an important hygiene rule – especially for young boys who could easily relieve themselves behind every tree, bush, or weed!

Normally, these campouts were in May when the weather was still somewhat cool. One particular year it was extremely hot. The boys were all encouraged to drink plenty of water. On one occasion, during the heat of the day, one little boy approached me and said, with tears in his eyes, "Pata wandy, my tang is sor, I bit ito a cacus."

The translation is, "Pastor Randy, my tongue is sore; I bit into a cactus."

I looked at his tongue, and it was covered in cactus spines. I asked how this happened. He said, as best he could, that he was thirsty and bit into a cactus to get some water. Note to self, "Do not bite into the cacti" as one of the rules.

RA Camp

Beyond the overnight RA campout just down the road, we would load the kids up in the church van every year for a weeklong RA camp at Alto Frio Baptist Encampment in Leakey, TX. Kids from around the area descended on the camp, eagerly anticipating a week of fun and activity. At this camp, there were indoor bunks, a dining hall, and an outdoor covered sanctuary. The kids were also taught knot-tying, archery, compass orienteering, and overall outdoor skills.

The most powerful time was spent in Bible Study and Worship. One year, I was asked to be the camp pastor, meaning I would provide the messages for the kids each evening. Blake was a year too young (5 years old) to come to the camp, but he was given a special pass. Being the camp pastor allowed me to stay in one of the encampment hotel rooms rather than in the cabin with the rest of the boys. This was a major plus! And Blake was able to stay with me at night.

Mid-way through the week, I was preaching a message with the audience of young boys in mind. As I preached, some of the boys were fidgeting while others seemed to be truly soaking it in. These camps can be powerful experiences as the power of the Lord is evident. During my sermon, I noticed that Blake was especially tuned in and seemed a bit emotional. After the sermon, an invitation was offered. Several boys came forward, including Blake. I was thrilled that God was apparently working in his life, and my sermon somehow touched him to make a response. When it was his turn to speak to the pastor (his dad), I leaned down, looked him in the eye, and asked, "Blake, why are you coming down?"

With big crocodile tears, he replied, "I miss my mommy!" I gave him a pat on the head, told him that I missed her too, and to go sit down.

A couple of things I learned or was reminded of in this interaction. First, emotions can be tricky. Emotions, like tears, can appear to indicate something greater than they are. Sometimes they are shed just because we miss our mom! Second, it is important to seek clarity, especially at an invitation. The question, "Why are you coming" is important. During that same camp, during the invitation, I asked the question to one boy who seemed to be disturbed. "Why are you coming?" His response was, "I've got to use the bathroom!" Clarity, for children and adults, in all conversations and interactions is a great practice!

Running to the Store

"I'm going to run to the store." Those words can be oxymoronic. First of all, I am not running to the store; I am going to get in the car and drive to the store. Second, one could get the impression from that statement that this will be a quick trip, especially since the grocery store is in town, and the town is a small town. Like going to the Post Office,

I knew that a grocery store run was rarely a quick trip. Inevitably, I would run into (there I go again!) people when I walked into the store, walking around the store, and finally, walking out of the store. Each person gave a greeting, and a short conversation ensued.

Along with the conversations, two memories were unique to this small-town store. First, during certain times of the day, the floors were being polished with an industrial machine. This in itself is not unusual. Store cleanliness should be a high priority. The oddity of this polishing endeavor was the machine itself. It was gas-powered. I cannot claim to be an expert on air quality or OSHA standards, but I am fairly certain that a gas-powered machine spewing fumes and carbon dioxide cannot be a great idea! I am confident that the machine has run its course by now – hopefully replaced with an electric model.

The second unique quality, one that I had not experienced, even in Yorktown, was the very helpful store public address system. Before cell phones, if your spouse went to the store, and while he was on the way, you suddenly forgot to tell them, you were simply out of luck. You would do without or encourage them to go back to the store.

This was a reality unless your spouse (in my case, wife) knew the phone number of the store. I can think of a few times when I heard this message over the loudspeaker, "Randy Marshall, please come to the store office; your wife is on the phone.!"

Since one-third of the store knew the identity of Randy Marshall, I would sheepishly make the Walk of Shame to the main office with sympathetic eyes following me. Once on the phone, my conversation would basically be, "Yes....O...K."

I would then pick up the requested item and continue my shopping. The pinnacle of this public announcement phone debacle came one day when I was perusing aisle 9. The announcement went like this, "Randy Marshall, your wife called; you need more milk!" Apparently, Susie figured to eliminate the middle man in her messaging!"

After this event, we began writing lists.

Funeral Home Directors

As long as there are funeral homes, there will be funeral home directors. These men and women have dedicated their lives to caring for the remains of the deceased and grieving family members. Working with these dedicated people allows me to look "behind the curtain." Most are meticulous in details, wanting to ensure that everything has been taken into account.

They want light on the open casket, but not too much light. They make sure the minister is present. They give him a glass of water and try to keep him in one place so he doesn't wander off. They check the sound. They check the video. They check on the musician(s). With clockwork precision, they begin the service. For lack of a better term, for this portion of their duty, they are the wedding coordinator of the funeral.

In the three communities that I served, they were also homegrown. The main funeral home directors in each location were also owners or part owners of the "family business." Unlike larger cities where you may only see the director during times of grief, the funeral home directors were at the picnics, barbeques, football games, and church. They were part of the community.

On one occasion, the funeral home director joined a group of other friends to visit one of my church members in the hospital. They had all been big fishing buddies. The church member had been very ill, in and out of consciousness. Because of the hospital's rules on visitation in the ICU, only one or two people could enter the room at a time. Several took turns going in and came out saying that the man gave no response. When our local funeral director came out, he was all smiles. He said that his eyes immediately opened when he leaned over the bed and spoke to our sick friend. I gave a pastoral nod while, of course, thinking, if I was laying there and I heard you speaking, I would open my eyes as well!

Because pastors work closely with funeral home directors, they tend to develop a professional relationship. It was common to receive a Christmas gift such as a gift card or a poinsettia plant. In Stockdale, the director had a custom of giving local pastors a honey-baked ham. It was a nice gesture. He would come by the house, wish us a Merry Christmas and present us with a frozen ham.

One year, while I was at the funeral home for a viewing the day before the funeral, the director stopped me. He said, "Preacher, while you are here, let me get your ham."

Now, in my mind, I knew that because he and his wife actually lived in the same building, he was going to his home freezer to retrieve this ham. But in another part of my mind, the suspicious part, I envisioned him taking the ham out of the same freezer that "Mr. Smith" had just occupied. He came out and presented me with the cold, frozen former pig. I took it home and ate it. Hey, you can't look a gift ham in the mouth!

Here Kitty, Kitty

I have always appreciated help from friends in a time of need. Friends have been by my side when my children were born, at the funerals of both my father and mother, grieving with us in times of sorrow and rejoicing with us in times of grief. Friends have also been there for me in innumerable mundane circumstances.

One of these circumstances involved the use of a truck. My wife and I bought a mattress in San Antonio, some 20 miles from Stockdale. True to form (for me), I decided to save the delivery cost and ask one of my friends to borrow their truck.

One advantage of pastoring a church in a small town in South Texas is the abundance of trucks. So, I asked one of my parishioners who lived out in the country in a "gated community." I say this tongue-in-cheek because the gate connected two fence posts on a dirt road leading to their double-wide trailer. The couple was prototypical small-town Texan. They had a deep southern accent, five young children, raised chickens for eggs, voted Republican, and loved the Lord.

They also had a truck. So, when I asked to borrow the truck to pick up the mattress, they readily agreed and decided to bring it to the church office. So, with the truck in the parking lot and the wife, Nancy handing me the keys, I was grateful for the ability to use the truck for the afternoon.

As we talked in the parking lot, I faintly heard something underneath the chassis. I have been around enough trucks to recognize familiar chugs, pings, and gyrations. What I heard, however, was a faint meow.

"Nancy, is there a cat under there?" I asked incredulously.

"Yeah, I think so," she said nonchalantly. "We have a momma cat that had a litter of kittens. One of them must have climbed up under there."

Long pause. I innocently asked, "Don't you think we need to try to get him out of there?"

She shrugged and said, "Just drive down the road for a few miles; he will eventually fall out."

Immediately, my mind produced a mental picture of driving 70 miles an hour down Hwy 87 with the sounds of a kitten meowing just below my feet. I estimated about the time I hit the outskirts of San Antonio; the undercarriage would become so hot that the kitten would give up hanging on and then just fly out. All nine lives would have been expended with this one event.

I said, "Nancy, I can't do that. I am going to try and get him out."

She looked at me as if I was crazy; after all, it's just a cat. I got on my knees to take a look, cautiously, knowing that a scared kitten could immediately wrap his body and his claws into my face.

After getting on my back and looking toward the cab, sitting precariously on the frame, I could make out a trembling kitten with large, frightened eyes. Using my negotiating skills, I said, "Here, Kitty, Kitty, Kitty."

Understandably, he just looked and gave a weak meow. So, using my pastoral skills, I gently reached up to him to help him down. Like some of my other parishioners, his ears were drawn back, hissed, and he attempted to swat me with his suddenly outstretched claw. I came out from under the truck, somewhat exasperated. Nancy just gave me an "I told you so" look. I must admit, at this point, I wondered if her plan wasn't so bad after all.

I dismissed the image out of my mind and got a towel out of my car. Back under the truck, I approached the cat, threw the towel around the feline, found the nap of his neck, and pulled him out despite his objections. I handed the ball of fur to a somewhat bemused Nancy. Mission accomplished.

While driving the truck down the road, I felt good that I had acted upon my ethical principles while also wondering if one of his brothers was still hiding beneath me.

Just a thought.

How many of our world picture the presence of God in the same way that a scared cat pictures a helping hand reaching to save him from a certain death? They are stuck in a hopeless situation. The only available saving power is able and ready to provide a saving hand. How many of us fought, hissed, and scratched at the hand of God only to realize that He did not desire to crush us but to save us? I can picture the kitten safely back at his home (assuming Nancy took it home) with a story to tell.

Hide and Seek

I have always tried to keep family central. I didn't want to be one of those pastor-dads that the kids grew up resenting because he was never around. The schedule of the small-town pastor allowed me to be at most of Blake and Amanda's activities. Susie and I attended Amanda's dance recitals, little-league softball and soccer games, and countless practices. We went to Blake's little-league baseball and school football games and more practices. We drove them to countless activities they participated in: swimming lessons, piano lessons, school play days, birthday parties, pool parties, the annual Stockdale Watermelon jubilee, the rodeo, Chuck-E-Cheese pizza; the list goes on and on.

On "normal" days, when I was home, we would play games, watch T.V., and hang out. Some days, one of the kids would say, "Let's play hide and seek!" It was usually Blake's idea.

For some reason, little Amanda didn't care for the idea of hiding in some small, dark confined space, wondering if anybody was really looking!" The game was relatively easy and short when the kids were younger (4 and 5 years old). The seeker would find the hider behind a chair, under a table, etc.

As the kids got a couple of years older, they got smarter, and the game became more challenging. Blake would even preplan his strategy long before we played, preparing some obscure closet location he could squirm into. To add some excitement and raise the difficulty level, we began turning off most of the lights in the house (the church parsonage.)

During one memorable hide-and-seek, I was the seeker, and Susie and the kids were hiding. As was the custom, I found Amanda first, and she was helping me find the other two. Though the confines of the search were in the house, I had genuine difficulty finding both.

Though Blake regularly stumped us, Susie had found a place as well. She had somehow found a way to hide between the curtains and the window in the master bedroom. Understand, the window in the bedroom did not extend to the floor. Like a hind deer on a sheer mountainside, she was managing to cling on the two-inch ledge. To fit in the window space, her head was cocked to one side as she faced the inside of the room. This was not the most comfortable position, but this was an excellent hiding place for my thin, agile wife.

Things were going well until she realized that car lights were shining on her back from the street in front of the house. She hoped they would go away because the silhouette on the curtain would give away her hiding spot. She was relieved when after several seconds, the car sped away. Shortly after, car lights were shining on her back again, though the lights were brighter this time – two cars!

Why are these people parked in front of our house? To her horror, she suddenly realized what they were seeing – a woman suspended from a window with her head cocked to one side! In the First Baptist Church parsonage! Willing to concede her great hiding spot, she immediately jumped off the window seal and turned the lights in the house back on. The game was over. Surprisingly no one knocked on our door, the police never showed, and the deacons didn't make a visit.

We lived in Stockdale for several years after this event. We never did find out who was behind the wheel that night. We never mentioned it. No one ever asked. Some things are better left unsaid.

The Intruder

Susie and I took a group of senior adults to Branson, Mo. For the uninformed, Branson is the senior adult destination of choice to hear old-time country and Gospel music. Some of the music is good; some is a bit cheesy.

We were having a great time in Branson while Grandma (Susie's mom) had graciously agreed to watch the kids, both now elementary school age. We stocked up on food and needed supplies. Amanda had recently had a birthday right before we left, so there was still birthday cake to eat. Blake assured us that he would take care of things and "not to worry about them." Everything ran smoothly at home until, one morning, before one of our breakfast buffets in Branson, we received a call from Grandma. She said in a very deliberate tone. "I just want you to know that everything is fine, just in case you get a call."

I learned a long time ago that when someone says, "Everything is fine," before you ask, "How is everything going?" then everything is not fine!

Here is the story, the best I could piece it together. On Wednesday night, Joyce (Grandma) and the kids were in the living room watching T.V. Suddenly, they heard something in the master bedroom. They turned down the volume on the T.V. All three listened to the strange noise coming from down the hall. It was a rustling sound as if someone was tearing up things.

The kids were wide-eyed. Grandma, being a former military wife, sprang into action. She cautiously began walking down the hall as the noise became more pronounced. She could see shadows as if some crazy person was ransacking the room. Immediately, she gathered the kids and ran outside. Right across the street was a neighbor, Barbara, who saw the terrified look of the trio and asked them what was going on. Someone was in the house, and they were tearing it apart! She went in to tell her husband, Ron. He walks out with a determined look and a loaded shotgun!

Now picture this scene with me. It was a perfect convergence. Right when Ron walks across the street with his shotgun, The First Baptist Church, Stockdale, Wednesday night prayer meeting is finishing. The group walks out the door, hears the story, and silently prays a bit more.

A larger crowd begins to gather. Imaginations begin to run wild. Perhaps someone was in the back thinking, "I remember seeing someone hanging in the window in that same room!"

Who knows what happens in that preacher's house? Ron stealthily opens the front door and walks in, shotgun in hand. The crowd grows a bit bigger. After about three agonizing minutes, Ron walks out of the house, shotgun in one hand, the culprit in the other. Ron had a big smile on his face. The feared "culprit" was a group of six mylar helium balloons, relics from Amanda's birthday party that had gotten caught in the room's ceiling fan! Somehow, they had floated down the hall into the master bedroom. The strings of the balloons had become entangled in the whirling fan blades.

This was the source of the rustling sound and the shadowy figure. The situation was explained when Ron exited the house, and the mystery was solved. Joyce was both relieved and mortified that the culprit was less sinister than imagined. The crowd began to disperse. People gave Joyce a compassionate look and a pat on the back. Joyce thanked Ron for his heroics, took the now battered balloons, and walked back into the house with the kids closely behind. On this day, at least, a disaster was diverted. Everything was fine. If memory serves me correctly, the event in Stockdale on this night was much funnier than any story I heard on the stages of Branson.

Pray For Peace

As the church grew, it became apparent more space was needed. The leadership determined that a separate building adjacent to the current facility was needed to provide Sunday School space and a larger Fellowship Hall. Among Texas Baptists, the Texas Baptist Men provided one of the great ministry programs. In communities like Stockdale, where new construction can be a financial strain, they assist in a powerful way.

The host church provides the building's foundation and all the construction materials on site. The Texas Baptist Men then arrive from across Texas in their travel trailers with their wives accompanying them. With military precision, they frame the building in one week and install sheetrock. The church provides one meal a day for their efforts. The men and women blessed the congregation and the community with their presence and incredible work.

One moment that stood out for me was a conversation with one of the men. He shared how, years ago, he had been diagnosed with an aggressive form of leukemia. Understandably, the news was devastating for him and his family. He shared that for weeks, he prayed for healing. Nothing seemed to change during that period, and his physical, mental, and spiritual energy waned. He relayed that one day, his prayer changed. He began to pray for peace. He figured it was a win-win prayer. As a believer, he knew that healing would indeed come, either on earth or in heaven. He knew that Jesus would be with him no matter where the path may lead. That brought him comfort and peace.

Obviously, healing on earth did come, but he had reached a spiritual rest that did not hinge on the outcome.

I have often thought of this conversation and tried to apply it to my life and family. I have heard others echo similar statements, usually coming from our senior adults who know more years are behind them than in front. May we live in His presence and experience the peace of God, a peace that is beyond all understanding.

The Association

Part of the life of the Baptist Pastor is his involvement in the local Baptist Association. The Association is a group of Baptist churches, sometimes county-wide, sometimes multi-county-wide, that voluntarily join together for shared efforts, fellowship, etc. I always liked Associational meetings and events because they allowed me to connect and reconnect with other pastors and widen my aperture of ministry.

Of course, like any fine Baptist institution, there are meetings. In both Yorktown and Stockdale, these were monthly meetings. So, just about every month, I and a group of people, normally elderly ladies, in the church would load up into the church van and travel to one of these meetings. The monthly meeting was always held in one of the Association's churches.

It was the host church's responsibility to provide meeting space in the sanctuary and prepare a meal beforehand, another fine Baptist tradition! We would eat the meal served, fellowship together, compliment the ladies in the kitchen and then have our hour-long meeting, which contained business and a program. Before I continue, please note that the people who attended these meetings were fine, outstanding men and women—pastors, staff members, and leading members of their respective congregations.

One particular meeting night, Susie and I had an appointment in San Antonio. Rather than drive back to Stockdale and turn around to drive back to the meeting location, we decided to drive there directly. Because she was not properly dressed for a fine Gambrell Associational meeting, she had brought her dress, pantyhose, and shoes to change into. We were running a bit late from our trip to San Antonio, so she dressed in the car on the way. Since this would save time and we were several miles away from the city limits of Stockdale, I thought it was a good idea.

After some maneuvering, she put on her dress, pantyhose, and shoes. All was well. Just as she finished touching up her makeup in the rearview mirror, I drove up to the church building. Being a friendly sort, she got out of the car and waved to a couple of cars, making their way into the parking lot. As I walked around the car to walk in with her, one of the drivers in the passing car, a pastor that I knew, slowed the car considerably and took an extra long look at my wife. My wife is a beautiful woman, but come on, show some tact! What would his wife say? Then I noticed that his wife, sitting next to him, also had an odd and peculiar look toward my wife.

When I finally got to her side of the car, Susie was closing the door, and I saw what they saw. In her haste to get dressed, she had tucked the back of her dress into her pantyhose. The front of the dress looked fine, but the back side was showing her backside. Being the conscientious husband I am, I immediately let her know! We both stood by the car as she pulled the dress to its proper place. I told her that it could have been worse. She could have walked around like that all night if I wasn't there to tell her. Her red face just glared at me.

Again, no one ever spoke to us about this. Apparently, what happens in the parking lot of an Associational Meeting stays in the parking lot!

Funny Things Happen at Funeral Homes

Back to the funeral home. Funny things can happen at a funeral. Though the words "funny" and "funeral" seem to be worlds apart, any time people are involved, "funny" things can happen. Sometimes the funny thing is not really funny in the ha-ha way but funny in the strange and unexpected way.

During one funeral, I hardly flinched when the family brought the deceased woman's dog, a chihuahua, to the funeral. I even agreed with the family's wishes to include little Rover in the obituary as one of the survivors. I admit, I was a bit surprised that when they filed past the casket, one of the family members placed the frightened dog on the deceased's chest, causing the little canine to spin around in panic. Who would have known? I was just glad that it wasn't a Great Dane.

Over the years, I learned that each family had a way of uniquely honoring the deceased in song, both through recorded songs and audio/video tributes. I distinctly remember a young lady singing Neil Diamond's "Sweet Caroline." When she got to the "bom, bom, bom" part of the song, she had the crowd sing along with her. Very touching.

Whether I knew the family very well or not, I would always meet with them a day or two before the funeral, which was normally a couple of days past the family member's death. A couple of times, a family member apologized about the unexpectant death, "I'm sorry that we couldn't give you more warning." That was like apologizing to the firefighter who just put out the fire in their house, "Sorry, we didn't expect to have a short in our wiring."

Sometimes people die. It's not something you can put in your planner. We would always talk about the deceased and what made them unique. After one daughter told a rather embarrassing story about her mother, the other daughter said, "She would just die if we told that!"

Now that was funny.

My First Wife

As stated earlier, one of the realities of being a small-town church pastor is the realization that life will be lived in a fishbowl. People notice the kind of car you drive. They are aware of the type of clothes you (and your wife and kids) wear. People listen to your every word, even words spoken in the heat of a high school football game. A wise pastor will be aware of the dynamic but not let it control his life. Watching what you say also applies to the words you say in your own home (the parsonage).

One particular event comes to mind. Susie and I were planning a night out. Another couple would accompany us, so we met at our house. The high-school-age babysitter for the evening was the daughter of one of our deacons. We all chatted for a few minutes, and then we were on our way.

After a few hours, we returned, paid the babysitter, and she went home. There was, however, an unresolved comment that needed to be addressed. The young girl's mother called my wife and asked her a very direct question: "Has Bro. Randy been married before?"

My wife was caught a bit off-guard and asked why she would think that. She replied that her daughter had overheard Susie comment about my (Randy's) golf clubs and that "his first wife had given him those."

Susie chuckled and said, "his first wife did give him the golf clubs; it was me. I am his first and only wife!"

Susie's attempt to be humorous had caused a stir. I can only imagine the conversation in the car on the way home. I can hear the conversation between this deacon's wife and her husband. Something like, "he could have been married before. We never really asked." Or, "I wonder if those are Susie's kids?" Or, "How many times has he been married, and why would Susie let him use those clubs?"

I don't know about any conversation and how far the rumor traveled. I do know that we were able to set the record straight. It also served as a reminder of words spoken, even in jest, and how much impact they can have.

Friday Night Miracle

Small-town Texas and Friday Night High School Football games go hand in hand. Friday Night football is more than a game; it is an event. Often, the highlight of the week for the community. Though other sports are played during the years – baseball, basketball, soccer, track, volleyball, etc., in Texas, football is king. Students are involved – those on the team, cheerleaders, pep squad, band, and students in the stands, including Junior Varsity football team members who played the night before. Adults are involved – parents, grandparents, and great-grandparents. Some are in the stands, some in the concession stand, and some on the field.

During home games, the town shuts down. Businesses that have store windows with shoe polish that says, "Go Brahmas, beat the Tigers!" are shuttered. The streets are empty. Pity the poor church that has planned some event on Friday Night! Friday Night Football is a cultural phenomenon. It is also the site of the miraculous. I have witnessed this myself.

As in any church, in Yorktown and Stockdale particularly, some of our senior adults could not venture outside their houses to attend church services. They were weak and frail. But on Friday nights, I would witness the miraculous. These dear saints who could not come to worship on a Sunday Morning and sit in a temperature-controlled sanctuary in a comfortable pew could navigate the stairs leading to the metal stands and sit on a hard, freezing cold or red-hot metal bench. During the game, they became animated with loud, healthy voices cheering their team and complaining to the referee. Their eyes were wide with excitement and fervor.

When I first witnessed this, I was ecstatic! The Lord had worked in a marvelous way! This dear saint had become alive and animated! Sadly, the team-clad senior adult had a relapse on Saturday and was not able to come on Sunday morning. This activity was repeated throughout the Fall season, even in out-of-town games.

Another observation I made about these senior adults and others who attended was the resiliency to brave the elements. I have been to games where the stands were full and remained full, despite 20-degree weather, with a blowing wind and even a driving rain. Their dedication and resiliency were remarkable. I could not help (actually, I could help it, but I harbored the thought) observe that I or the church did not have this kind of influence. I could imagine announcing an outdoor service with a prediction of cold and rain. I could hear people say, "Pastor, we need to cancel that service. No one would dare come out on a night like this."

"Yes," I could reply, "no one in their right mind would come out on a night like this…unless they saw some value in it."

I know the draw on Friday Nights is not just football players on the field. It's not just the cheerleaders and the pep squad. It's not just the members of the band. Parents, grandparents, and great-grandparents give their time and risk their health for one reason; these students are family – children, grandchildren, and great-grandchildren. They go to great lengths to lovingly support them. They applaud and encourage them as they participate in something bigger than themselves. A strong bond and connection exists in being a part of a shared event.

Let us always be that involved in both our children and youth. And let us particularly be willing to carry that excitement and engagement

The Marshall Chronicles

from the Friday Night Lights to Sunday Morning Worship - sharing valuable family moments with those we love.

Goose 911

What do you do when a goose is on the loose? Normally, nothing until a problem arises. Stockdale had its share of roaming animals, particularly dogs and cats, but unlike most communities, we also had a roaming goose. Most days, he wasn't much of a bother; until the puppy incident.

This incident reminded me of old Dragnet episodes: "The story you about to see (hear) is true. The names have been changed to protect the innocent. This is the city, and most residents are respectable and upstanding. Nothing much ever happens. But in the dark recesses of the early morning, an uncommon situation occurred that required a swift response..."

One of our neighbors down the street, we will call her Mary, had purchased a puppy. It was delivered in a crate. The owner of the puppy decided to keep it in the crate on the porch until the dog was acclimated to his new home. Unfortunately, the whining puppy attracted and apparently annoyed the goose.

In the darkness of pre-dawn, Mary heard a commotion on her porch. She came outside and found the goose attacking her dog. This large bird took an unconventional approach by attempting to choke the puppy by putting its long neck down his throat. This surprising tactic worked, and the dog was in danger of suffocation. In defense of her dog, Mary eventually dislodged the goose with a broom. But, the goose was relentless. He kept coming back, obsessed with eliminating the terrified puppy.

Out of desperation, Mary called 911. This was plan A.

Reports of the account state that the conversation went something like this:

Operator – 911, what's your emergency?

Caller – (Frantic voice) Help, my dog is getting attacked by a goose!

Operator – (Pause) Ma'am, did you say that your dog is getting attacked by a goose?

Caller – Yes! Please send somebody now!

Operator – I'm sorry, I can't help you; you may want to call the zoo (click)

Plan B.

Stockdale didn't have an organized police department, but there was a guy that the Wilson County Sheriff's Department had deputized to maintain order. We will call him Joe – Joe Friday. So she called him, and he immediately responded. Though the county 911 operator did not see the danger, the local deputy quickly realized the goose/dog/woman dilemma and took immediate action.

Upon arrival, he found the woman on the porch, frantically attempting to shoo the goose with a broom. The woman was screaming, the dog whimpering, and the goose with raised wings honking. After ascertaining the situation, the deputized officer decided to take it to the next level. With authority, he whacked the head of the goose with the back of a shovel. With a now dizzy goose, the situation was under control. For those concerned, the goose experienced no permanent harm!

No other authorities were called. No arrests were made. To my knowledge, the goose got off with just a warning.

As this episode fades, follow-up lessons are learned:

The woman learned that the 911 system will not answer to a goose-on-dog attack.

The puppy learned not to open his mouth around a goose. This lesson became obsolete when the dog grew up to weigh around 150 pounds.

The goose learned that just because you can do something doesn't mean you should.

Joe Friday learned that a shovel has multiple functions.

The author learned that just about any memory can be included in a book!

Cue Dragnet theme song.

Out of Chicken

Being a Baptist minister and having a love for chicken seem to go hand in hand. So, on a Thursday afternoon, on our way back to Stockdale from a trip to San Antonio, Susie and I decided to go through the drive-thru and pick up some chicken at a restaurant specializing in Fried Chicken. Driving into the parking lot, I saw pictures of fried chicken – sandwiches, nuggets, platters. Even though it was only 4:00 p.m., I began to lick my Baptist lips in anticipation.

I drove to the drive-thru lane and stopped firmly in front of the large neon menu that contained more pictures of chicken and various menu options. In the middle of the window was a speaker/microphone. The voice of a woman located inside the building at the end of the drive-thru lane pleasantly asked, "May I help you?"

I said, "Yes, I would like the family chicken meal."

The voice on the other end said, "Sir, I'm sorry, but we are out of chicken."

I looked at the big chicken logo and glanced at the chicken picture on the oversized menu plastered on the glass of the actual building. I intently stared at the faceless speaker/microphone and slowly and deliberately inquired, "Is this a restaurant that sells chicken?"

"Yes Sir," came the reply.

I continued, "And you have no chicken?"

I could understand them being out of mashed potatoes, corn on the cob, biscuits, napkins, but chicken? I looked at my wife. She shrugged. I took my foot off the brake, merged out of the drive-through line, and slowly glared at the passing window. Inside, two others were curiously watching me as well.

Let me expand on this "out of chicken, out of body experience."

Do you ever think that people walk up to our places of worship expecting to find church, a place where God's people authentically meet to hear a Word from God while joyfully worshipping with a sense of unity and purpose, and walk away sadly disappointed? They see the sign out front that says, "church," they come to a building that says "church," and they are handed a bulletin that says "church." They may see a cross, stained glass, pews, and a steeple. They may hear music from a choir or band, words from a preacher, or maybe even a greeting from an usher. The sights and sounds of church are all around, but are they undeniably experiencing a Spirit-filled, Bible-based, God-honoring time of worship? Do they leave just as spiritually hungry as when they arrived, or have they been fed and challenged by the transformational truth of the Word of God? Do they see all the outward trappings of church but remain spiritually hungry?

Though we cannot guarantee that the seed of the Gospel will take root in the individual seeker, the church should always be the church. (BTW, I know you are wondering, yes, we did go somewhere else that had chicken! Lesson learned – never deny chicken to a hungry Minister!)

New Doors!

In addition to the new building, we were also able to repair, re-structure, and refurbish the Sanctuary. The 1950's era theatre seats had seen better days. Updates to the sound system and furniture were long overdue. The windows needed to be replaced. The interior of the Sanctuary was about to be transformed. In January 1997, I wrote the following:

"Have you heard? The church is getting new doors. When those new doors open, you will walk on new carpet into a refurbished foyer. The Sanctuary walls will be freshly painted with a new ceiling illuminated with new lights. You will then sit in new pews ready to Worship with improved sounds coming from the new sound system. Your eyes will be directed to the stage area where the new pulpit, Lord's Supper table, columned front, and restructure walls direct your attention to the baptistry where new Stained Glass windows shine forth as a backdrop drawing us into His presence.

"Whew! Sounds like something our church would need in the 21st Century. Actually, those plans are for the next century, and the future begins this month. As the New Year dawns, changes will take place that will have an effect upon the worshippers at the First Baptist Church for the next 50 years. These renovations will open new doors to a new look. The doors will open inward to invite worshippers to praise and adore our Go. The doors will open outward to challenge worshippers to go and tell the Good News. The doors open to the young and the old, for our generation and the ones to come. True to its theme, the Sanctuary Renovation project will be 'Opening New Doors for Generations to Come!'"

The congregation fully embraced the changes. For six weeks, we met in the Fellowship Hall for Sunday Worship. Because of the artistry of the stained-glass windows, it took a total of 10 months to complete this phase of the project. Clear glass was initially installed, and slowly, each of the stained-glass masterpieces was put into place.

Combined, the windows portrayed the major themes of God's Word, from the days of creation to the glories of the Resurrected Jesus and the giving of the Holy Spirit. It was and is a breathtaking site and remains a place where the beauty of the structure matches the spiritual beauty of the people inside who worship a God who deserves our best.

Watermelon Jubilee

Since 1937, on the third weekend in June, residents of Stockdale and the surrounding area enjoy the Stockdale Watermelon Jubilee. As advertised, it is one of the oldest watermelon festivals in Texas and is a refreshing slice of summertime fun! The jubilee includes plenty of watermelons, a parade (complete with a celebrity Grand Marshal), food vendors, a rodeo, entertainment, and carnival rides. It's a big event that is held annually in the city park.

Children enjoy the carnival rides that have been hastily set up. Parents, who are normally very cautious concerning the safety of their children, throw that caution to the wind. They don't think twice about placing their child on a whirling contraption of questionable reliability under the supervision of a man who looks shady at best. It's all good!

Along with the food, there are also drinks. For the uninformed, traditionally, Baptists don't drink alcohol, at least not in public! But during the jubilee, like the safety of their children, caution is thrown to the wind. Many times I have approached one of my church members holding a beer. With eyes wide, they attempt to put the beer behind their back or casually to the side. This action used to make me uncomfortable, simply knowing that I was making them uncomfortable. Over time, I saw this action as humorous. I once asked one of my parishioners, "If you are comfortable drinking your beer before God, why do you think you need to hide it from me? His matter-of-fact answer was, "God is more forgiving than you are!" Ouch!

A common practice of beer drinkers, especially in the hot, south Texas summers, was to carry the can in a koozie. A koozie is a can-shaped insulated sleeve that helps keep the drink, in this case, the beer cooler. Koozies come in different colors and often have some sports or business logo emblazoned on the side. One style of koozie has a camouflaged design. I guess this is designed for the hunter to match his outfit to camouflage his presence. Deer, like ministers, can spot shiny objects in the wild.

In examining these koozies, it occurred to me that if I was a member of the First Baptist Church with a beer in my hand, and I saw my pastor coming toward me, I would want to have one of these camouflaged koozies, or what I would call an emergency beer concealer. When the minister or the nosy deacon approaches, place your hand into the nearest bush, and the concealment is complete!

Proverbs 28:13 says, "People who conceal their sins will not prosper, but if they confess and turn from them, they will receive mercy."

As believers, we must look through the lens of the Word of God and determine if the things we feel guilty about or try to hide are in the category of "sins." If it is a gray area, maybe the question should be, "Is it right for me?" Or "How will this help or hinder my witness?" If we determine what we think or do is spiritually unhealthy, the best response is to give it to God and allow Him to direct us.

Balancing Godly attitude and behavior with societal and/or church expectations can be tricky. One thing is certain; our spiritual lives should be an open book for all to see. We should be honest in all we do, even when the pastor shows up!

A Farewell

Saying farewell to Stockdale was one of the hardest things we have ever done. After eight and a half years, we were a part of the community. Below are the words I wrote in the January 1998 Church Newsletter:

"I thank my God every time I remember you. In all my prayers for all of you, I always pray, with joy because of your partnership in the gospel from the first day until now, being confident of this, that He who began a good work in you will carry it on to completion until the day of Christ Jesus." Philippians 1:3-6

As most of you know, after much prayer and seeking the Lord's will, I have accepted the pastorate of the First Baptist Church of Dickinson. My resignation here in Stockdale will be effective January 4th. Words cannot fully express the heaviness of heart that has accompanied this decision. Our family's desire is to simply walk in obedience to His will, and we have determined this is His leading. Like Paul, as he thought of the church in Philippi, I thank God for each of you and the richness that you have brought to my life and my family. Thank you for...

Loving us for ourselves

In our eight years, you never tried to make us into a former pastor's family, but simply allowed us to be ourselves. You loved us even when I said a blunder in the pulpit, when Susie wore her crazy sunglasses, and when our kids acted like kids. You saw us not as an extension of the church building, but as an extension of your own family.

Allowing me to lead

I know it wasn't easy letting a young, idealistic 29 year old lead. You, however, made it easy for me. Together, we built a new education/fellowship hall building and renovated the sanctuary. We participated in outreach ministries such as area-wide Scripture distributions, worship services in the city park, and clothing drives. We discussed and rehashed ideas so that we could be effective in our community and world. Let's face it, some of the ideas I had were not so great! You gave me the freedom to fail so we could discover new ministries that would work.

Letting me expand

I'm not talking about my waist! You allowed me to expand by encouraging me to attend conferences and retreats that have deepened my faith and broadened my mind. Thanks for allowing me to participate in the Air Force Reserve and seeing it as a mission field and not just being away from the church.

Being a friend

Even pastors need friends. Thanks for involving me and my family in your world – not just your "church world" but in play and gatherings with family and friends.

Hurting with us

Obviously, in eight years, we have shared moments of grief together. I was able to be by your side as you faced sadness, pain, and uncertainty. It was a sacred honor to have witnessed with the the last breath of your loved ones, to comfort, and to lead in the funeral service. Ministry of Presence has also come my way. When my father died, our family was overwhelmed with cards, food, and other expressions of concern. Many of you traveled to San Antonio on a weekday to attend a funeral of a man you had never met, in order to show your support. That same love was shown at the death of Susie's brother. You have shown over and over that your love is overflowing.

All the fun times of ministry together

Who says you can't have fun at church?! We will remember the Youth camps, RA camps, GA camps, Vacation Bible Schools, Football Fellowships, Super Bowl parties, Marriage Retreats, Six Flags Trips, the Branson trip, Christmas and Easter Musicals, Sunday School parties and countless Fellowships. Unexpected occurrences in Worship, many that came from a child's mouth during the children's sermon or during the sermon itself, could fill a book. Memories of Weddings, Anniversaries, Baptisms and other celebrations will always be close to our hearts.

Thanks for all the memories and the opportunity to serve. Your imprint is indelibly placed upon us, no matter where we may go, no matter where I minister. We are still co-workers together.

Paul continued by writing, "Being confident of this that He who began a good work in you will carry it on to completion until the day of Christ Jesus." Ministry is not a sprint, it is a marathon. Despite the obstacles, disappointments, or setbacks, we are called to strive forward. It may be in Stockdale, it may be in Dickinson, it may be across the world. Let me encourage you to keep developing the faith that God has placed within you. Though our relationship as Pastor family and congregation has changed, our love and friendship have not. Each of you has an open invitation to visit when you are in the Galveston area. We certainly will return to visit. My prayers are with you as you begin your search for a new pastor. Whomever God calls to Stockdale will be fortunate because I know the congregation that awaits him and his family. The best days of First Baptist church are still ahead! Keep striving forward and fulfilling the desires of His heart as you seek His will together.

Dickinson, TX
1998

Another New Beginning

Mid-way between Houston and Galveston off I-45 and FM 517 sits the city of Dickinson. In 1824, John Dickinson received a land grant from the Mexican government for the area just north of the present-day location of Dickinson in Galveston County. Though still possessing a small-town atmosphere, Dickinson was much more urban than Yorktown and Stockdale.

It was situated between Texas City to the south, a city that employed thousands of workers in the petrochemical industry. To the north was the famed Johnson Space Center. Both the town and the church were a combination of individuals in blue-collar and white-collar jobs. Vocations ranged from oil refinery workers, teachers, and clerks, all the way to NASA employees. Saying, "That's not rocket science," took on a brand-new meaning.

Dickinson definitely had a different demographic, but the needs were the same. People needed to be exposed to the love and grace of Jesus. Believers were still in need of discipleship. Various ministry and mission opportunities abounded.

Vocationally, a big change for me was the ability to work with a full-time staff. The youth minister recently graduated from the University of Mary-Hardin Baylor. He was also newly married. He was a full-time minister and a part-time seminary student.

There were also two full-time secretaries – an office secretary and a financial secretary. In addition, the church had a part-time music minister and later a part-time children's minister. The church also had a full-time children's weekday preschool program director. Having a church staff was appealing to greater enable us to coordinate a variety of intergenerational ministries.

Let's get started!

Home

For our family, a plus of being in Dickinson was the ability to buy our own home. In our previous two churches, we lived in a church-owned parsonage. The advantage of a parsonage is that all repairs and updates are the church's responsibility. The other advantage is not worrying about financial market fluctuations in home buying and selling. As in Yorktown, when we left Stockdale, we simply loaded up and left without any need to worry about the sale of a home.

The biggest disadvantage of a parsonage, of course, is the inability to build equity. Time in ministry flies. Just over the horizon is retirement. Not having a place to go after retirement can be a major concern. Churches love us and see the need to support their pastor; however, when retirement comes, they pat us on the back, give us a big thanks, and maybe a little going-away gift. They then move on, preparing for the next pastor. So, the ability to buy a house was a major plus.

Susie and I could not find a house that met our needs. We ended up renting for six months and having a new home built – another new experience full of ups and downs. In the rental home, we put only the bare minimum in the house, knowing that we would be moving again. The garage was full of boxes.

After we moved to the new house, one of the new coaches at the Jr. High and his wife bought the house we were renting. One day, with a wry smile, he said he had found my "stash." I looked at him, a bit dumbfounded. He described a drawer in the guest bathroom. I knew which drawer he was referencing. We never could get it open. Apparently, it was stuck closed because of an obstruction inside the drawer. The obstruction was a bag of marijuana! I assured him it wasn't mine!

Come to think of it; I never asked what he did with that bag.

Living Water Works

Inspiration can come from a water bill!

One morning I read in my water bill and subsequently from our local paper that the Dickinson Water District was celebrating its 60th anniversary. I also noted that First Baptist Church, Dickinson, was also celebrating its 60th anniversary. This began a theme of discussion and a sermon series entitled "Living Water Works!"

In the same 60-year period that the Dickinson Water District had been providing life-sustaining fresh water, the First Baptist Church has been sharing eternal life-sustaining water to the Dickinson community. One passage shared was John 4:13-14: To the woman at the well, Jesus said, "Everyone who drinks of this water shall thirst again; but whoever drinks of the water that I shall give him shall never thirst; but the water that I shall give him shall become in him a well of water, springing up to eternal life."

As I stated then, "Our purpose for the last 60 years has been to allow the living water to spring up within us and spring out to our thirsty community. As we reflect on the wave of memories, we crest toward the future anticipating new heights. In light of this, our theme for the next three months is 'Living Water Works!'"

The theme was well-received as we began our ministry together. The only negative is that our area experienced an overabundance of rain during these three months! We held our annual church picnic in the fall at a local park. It included a barbeque, potato salad, other sides, table games, a football game, and a youth/adult softball game. This year's picnic included rain. No one likes rain at a picnic; however, one of my favorite memories that year was the fun we had in the falling rain and the resulting puddles. We were all soaked but had smiles on our faces. I have a picture to prove it!

We had fun because we decided to have fun despite the elements and even more fun because of the elements. Much of ministry at Dickinson was like this – meaningful ministry despite cloudy, rainy skies. I mean, let's face it – Living Water Works!

PR

Allow me to focus on the youth of the church once more. As a pastor, I have regularly interacted with the church youth. At Yorktown and Stockdale, I was both Pastor and, by default, Youth leader and Youth Camp counselor. It was my job to drive the church bus to the camp and spend the week with them as one of their counselors. We worshipped, played, ate camp food, laughed, and cried together. The ability to get away from their everyday lives and experience the joy of youth camp was invaluable.

As mentioned, the church was blessed with a full-time Youth Minister, Mike Murrie. We served together for almost ten years. As the Youth Minister, Mike was responsible for all the youth ministries. He was and is a role model for my children as they grew into young adulthood. Though Mike was the face of FBC Youth Ministry, I was still able to interact with these Jr. High and High School students regularly.

Young people have a unique sensitivity to the movement of God. For many, their hearts are open and pliable to the Gospel as they seek to live out their faith in the midst of both internal and external pressures. Unlike many youth groups, this group of young people would regularly sit on the front two or three rows, right in front of the pulpit. Now, most churchgoers, especially youth, will tell you that the premium seats in the church are toward the back. These youth were front and center, many taking notes (hopefully, most were taking notes of the sermon!)

On Sunday evenings, some of the older youth would often challenge me. They would give me a word to be used in my sermon. It was normally an obscure word like "albatross," "ambidextrous," "unequivocally," or "man-eater." Most times, the sermon's topic was far from this obscure word. I would incorporate the word something like this "God is love. Even when the world seems to be a bunch of man-eaters, God loves us."

I would purposely wait to use the magic word toward the end of the sermon (so they would keep listening!) When it was used, I never revealed the game to the rest of the congregation. Only the youth and I were in on it. I doubt that Charles Spurgeon or other preaching giants had this practice. Then again, I have heard some strange words come from pulpits!

One of my favorite memories of this time was a term of endearment given to me by our youth: "PR," short for "Pastor Randy." Whether on a mission trip, youth discipleship meetings in our home, "out to lunch bunch" at a local restaurant, school, football game, grocery store, or wherever, the greeting was the same – "Hey, PR!"

For these youth, including my own children, it was such a short period of time. My prayers are with each of these young people who are now young adults as they navigate their way through life. Hopefully, the years spent in church and the youth group have helped ground them in their faith while allowing them to soar!

Amazing Grace

Another FBC Youth story...

A long-standing practice at the First Baptist Church was a church-wide Sunday Night "Fifth-Sunday Singing" on months that had a 5th Sunday. This forum provided an opportunity for people to hone some of their musical abilities in front of a smaller and more informal setting than on a Sunday morning. It included those who were comfortable sharing their abilities and some who were more inexperienced. Some would sing a solo, some in a group. Others played instruments.

One Sunday, weeks preceding the upcoming 5th Sunday, a group of high school girls approached me and asked if they could perform an interpretive dance. At the time, interpretive dance had become somewhat popular in churches. Admittedly, this was a bit of a stretch for our more conservative congregation. I agreed. I figured it was just another form of religious expression that the congregation would appreciate. Also, their enthusiasm was infectious, and I didn't want to dampen their spirit.

As the day approached, I became increasingly apprehensive of my immediate "yes." So, on this evening, after the conclusion of very appropriate church musical numbers, it was the girls' turn. They were the last to perform. Did I mention these girls were members of the Dickinson High School Drill Team?

Randy Marshall

Six young girls entered from the back of the sanctuary wearing what I would call their practice drill team outfits. Tight-fitting outfits that seemed appropriate hundreds of yards away from the stands at the football stadium suddenly seemed out of place on a close-up view on the stage of the First Baptist Church. Their "interpretive dance" seemed to me to be just another routine from their dance team, just set to contemporary Christian music.

I was sitting toward the front, in the middle of the sanctuary, sinking lower and lower in my seat. I wondered if the deacons would call a meeting immediately after the service. How would the older ladies respond to the giddy, smiling girls in their skimpy outfits? After all was complete, I was prepared for a confrontation. Sure enough, from the back of the sanctuary, five of our dear Senior Adults ladies made a bee-line to the girls.

What they did next was totally unexpected. Each of these dyed-in-the-wool church ladies embraced the girls, complimented them, and thanked them for sharing their talents. I was shocked! I know the outfits worn were questionable, the music they played was not the ladies' favorite genre, and the moves on the stage were not what they had ever seen on the stage. The ladies, however, seemed to look past all of those things and looked at the hearts of these young girls. They loved the girls as they were. They saw them as children of the king.

Nothing negative was said, no meetings were set. Just an intergenerational moment of Christian love.

It was truly an act of Amazing Grace!

National Events

The years 1999-2001 brought at least three events that garnered national attention. The first event was Y2K. Y2K was a threat, whether real or perceived, that predicted widespread confusion and anarchy caused by a common computer programming shortcut. Many computers only allowed two digits (99 instead of 1999.) As a result, there was panic that computers would be unable to operate at the turn of the millennium when the clock turned to the four-digit year 2000.

The doomsday predictions included a complete shutdown of computer systems and infrastructures, including banking, power plants, air traffic, etc. Some headed for the hills, away from civilization. Most just remained in place and hoped for the best. Whether because of intense computer programming changes or because the predictions were grossly overstated, January 1, 2000, came and went.

A second national event was on September 11, 2001, when a terrorist group hijacked four commercial passenger airplanes and carried out suicide attacks against targets in the United States. These attacks brought widespread fear and began a decades-long war. I was at my home preparing to go to the church office. As I watched the morning news, I saw the first plane hit one of the twin towers. Like most, I thought it was a terrible accident until I saw the second plane hit the south tower and then a third plane hit the Pentagon. Questions swirled about what was next. As most know, this event deeply hit our national psyche and continues to have wide-ranging repercussions.

The third national event occurred on February 1, 2003. The Space Shuttle Columbia disintegrated as it reentered the atmosphere over Texas and Louisiana, killing all seven astronauts on board. This accident was personal to many in our area who worked directly with the Space Shuttle program. After the disaster, Space Shuttle flight operations were suspended for more than two years. Construction of the International Space Station was paused until flights resumed in 2005.

Add to these disasters other national news and local tragedies of school shootings, economic downturns, traffic accidents, unsolved murders, and of course, occasional hurricanes and other natural disasters. All of these occasions cause people to stop and wonder, mourn and grieve, cry, and occasionally scream! In the middle of it all is the faith community that speaks in times like these.

God's Word can bring comfort. As we gathered in prayer, we would focus on passages like:

"God is our refuge and strength, an ever-present help in trouble. Therefore, we will not fear, though the earth gives way and the mountains fall into the heart of the sea, though its waters roar and foam and the mountains quake with their surging. There is a river whose streams make glad the city of God, the holy place where the Most High dwells, He says, 'be still and know that I am God; I will be exalted among the nations, I will be exalted in the earth'" (Psalm 46 1-4, 10-11).

or

"The Lord is my shepherd, I shall have no want, He makes me lie down in green pastures, He leads me beside quiet waters, He restores my soul. He guides me along the right paths for His name's sake. Even though I walk through the valley of the shadow of death, I will fear no evil for you are with me; your rod and your staff they comfort me. You prepare a table before me in the presence of my enemies. You anoint my head with oil; my cup overflows. Surely goodness and lovingkindness will follow me all the days of my life, and I will dwell in the house of the Lord forever. (Psalm 23)

or

Hundreds of other Bible verses that bring comfort during difficult times. God's Word speaks into our lives, and it truly is a privilege to be with those, individually and corporately, to speak words of truth and comfort as we experience life together.

Turning 40

In 2000, I turned 40. I know now that 40 is not old. But the turn from 39 to 40 seemed massive. It has been said that 30 is the old age of youth and 40 is the youth of old age. Yes, the youth of old age. In our newsletter in August of 2000, I wrote these words:

Consider this...throughout the Scriptures, the number forty has been a significant number. During the great flood, it rained 40 days and 40 nights. Isaac married Rebekah when he was 40 years old. The Hebrews wandered in the wilderness for 40 years. Joshua was 40 years old when he spied out the Promised Land. Moses spent 40 years in the palace, 40 years of preparation in the desert, and 40 years leading the people. The Philistines were in control of Israel for 40 years. Eli led Israel for 40 years. Soul reigned as King for 40 years. David also reigned for 40 years, as did Solomon. Solomon had 40 thousand horse stalls. The main hall in Solomon's temple was 40 cubits long. Elijah ate a meal that allowed him to make a journey of 40 days and 40 nights. Jonah warned the Ninevites that they had 40 days to repent. Jesus fasted 40 days and 40 nights. He was tempted in the desert for 40 days and spent 40 days on Earth after the resurrection.

Maybe turning 40 isn't so bad after all.

To my church family, thank you so much for your words of affirmation (and comfort), cards, and gifts as I turn this Scripturally significant year of birth. Thanks to those who took out a couple of hours of a precious Saturday afternoon to make my 40-year-old heart jump in surprise. It was a pleasure to celebrate with my church family.

Isaiah 40 reminds us that as we wait on the Lord we can soar with wings like eagles – certainly reassuring words to all of us old birds who still desire to fly high.

40 and still counting,
Randy

People Like George

Though most days do not bring national disaster or calamities (thankfully!), every day has its own set of challenges and opportunities - some planned, some unplanned. I would often drive to the office with a certain agenda in mind. Sometimes, the days went as planned. Other times, life events got in the way. I find that someone has been rushed to the hospital, a water leak needs attention, a staff member has an issue, a disgruntled church member drops to share their opinion, and a hundred other things.

And then, there is George. George is a real person (not his real name), and he represents a number of people that come our way, people that make you scratch your head and go, "Huh!"

George and his wife were not church members. They were members of the community at large. I don't believe they were homeless, but they had tendencies that would make you think they were. Their clothes and hair were unkept, they had a certain aroma, and they pushed a shopping cart through town. Though harmless, he reminded me of the old cartoon character, the Tasmanian Devil, when he entered a room. Occasionally, he would enter the church office.

To enter my office, a person would go through two rooms – the entry area, the secretary's office, and then my own. In my office, even when the door was closed, I knew when George had arrived. He was loud and a bit overbearing. He would begin to see office items such as a stapler, a pen, a stack of paper, and a brush in the lost and found. He would then ask, "Can I have this?"

The secretary would politely say, "No, George, you can't have that."

It was often then that his wife would say, just as loud and aggressively, at the top of her voice. "George! You can't have that!"

He would then want to come to my office and inquire about my desk items. I admit there was one time when I intentionally avoided him. My office had three modes of escape – the door to the secretary's office, a door next to it that led to the hallway, and a door by my desk that led to the parking lot. I was running late for an appointment, heard George, and immediately exited out the door. Others were in the office, so I knew my secretary wasn't left there alone. Nevertheless, she later expressed her displeasure at my sudden escape!

People like George are a challenge. I know that God loves them. In my mind, I know that they don't realize how they come across. Sometimes, people like George push a shopping cart, and sometimes they drive a Mercedes. Sometimes, their appearance is disheveled. Sometimes they are well-dressed and well-groomed. Their demeanor may be aggressive or a bit more passive or passive-aggressive. People like George are often self-focused and only see one way of doing things. They burst in and out of our lives without regard for their surroundings and little or no awareness of how they are perceived.

I know the best approach is not to simply appease them or escape through the back door. Though my patience sometimes wears thin, one approach I have taken with people like George is to help them slow down. Slow down their thoughts, slow down their actions, and at times be slow to speak and be slow to anger. I try to listen to them and encourage them to catch their breath and see the bigger picture. Most of all, people like George need a lot of love, the kind of love that only God can provide.

We should never allow them to run over us, invade our space and take our stuff. At the same time, we can treat them with respect. We will not be perfect in this, but let us treat people like George in the same way God treats people like us because, let's face it, sometimes God looks at us and sees us a bit disheveled as well!

Face-to-Face with the Right Stuff

My focus of this book is to share my experiences as a local church pastor. As noted, I also served as a Reserve Air Force Chaplain. More will be written about those experiences at a later time. Allow me to share one event while serving as Pastor in Dickinson.

In October 2004, I received a phone call asking if I could provide an invocation at a Memorial Service for a retired Air Force Officer. This was not the first time that I had received a call like this. However, the difference in this call was that it came from the commander's office at nearby Ellington Field. The Memorial Service was for former Air Force pilot and astronaut Gordon Cooper. I took a moment to soak in the request. Gordon Cooper was one of the seven original astronauts in Project Mercury, the first manned space effort by the United States in the early 1960s. The elite astronaut team became known as the "Mercury Seven" as well as the "Original Seven" and the less glamorous "Astronaut Group 1."

These men were chosen from hundreds of military test pilot applicants for their physical, mental, and emotional strength and stamina. Each had a genius-level IQ. After their selection, the seven were national heroes compared to explorers and innovators like Columbus, Magellan, and the Wright brothers.

Gordon Cooper was one of the youngest of the original seven. The world knew him as Leroy Gordon Cooper, Jr., a space pioneer who set endurance records in both his Mercury Faith 7 flight and his Gemini 5 mission. To his fellow astronauts and much of America, he was known as "Gordo."

The caller on the other end of the line was requesting that I represent the Air Force and join the three other surviving members of the "Mercury Seven" - Scott Carpenter, Wally Schirra, Congressman John Glenn – several high-ranking military members and the NASA community at the historic Johnson Space Center to pay tribute to this hero. To top it off, the memorial coincided with a gathering of Apollo astronauts, including Neil Armstrong and Jim Lovell.

After soaking in the question, I answered, "Yes, I would be honored to provide the invocation."

What an understatement! I was intrigued by living just a few miles south of the Johnson Space Center (JSC). As a kid, one of the pictures that hung in my room, even through high school, was a picture of the Apollo 11 crewmen Neil Armstrong, Buzz Aldrin, and Michael Collins. Armstrong became the first man to walk on the moon on July 21, 1969, fulfilling President John F. Kennedy's goal of reaching the moon before the Soviet Union by the end of the 1960s.

A significant number of residents of Dickinson had a connection with the space program, both as contractors and NASA employees. Hearing their stories and current progress was always thrilling for me. But now, I was asked to rub shoulders with these past and present giants of space exploration. So on Friday morning, October 15th, wearing my Air Force "Dress Blues," I drove through security at the Johnson Space Center to the gathering point. I was met by a command representative and driven to Teague Auditorium, where the ceremony would occur.

I was impressed with the organization of the event and the military precision of each detail. All participants in the ceremony gathered and entered onto the stage. Once situated, I took my seat beside John Glenn, who was seated next to the other two Mercury astronauts, who sat next to an Air Force General. The large auditorium was packed with NASA employees and invited guests. The intellectual energy in the room could have powered a small city! And then there was me.

Fortunately, this part of the story does not include something I said or did that I can laugh about now! The invocation was acceptable, and the memorial was meaningful. Cooper's fellow astronaut, Wally Schirra, said, "We seven were bonded like brothers, maybe even closer if that's possible."

John Glenn shared anecdotes about his friend. "Gordo has scrambled," he said, invoking the language of test pilots. "I'm sure we'll all rendezvous out there somewhere."

During the memorial service, Expedition 9 crewmembers Mike Fincke and Gennady Padalka paid tribute to Cooper from orbit, ringing the ship's bell on the International Space Station.

The second part of the day's events took us to an outdoor memorial site for a select few – only media and guests, including the chaplain. On the way to the new location, a group of us piled into a van. I get in with some other military members and then realize that two Mercury Seven astronauts, Wally Schirra and Scott Carpenter, ride with us. Wally sits next to me. It seemed odd to me to see them riding in a van. I expected them to be transported in some ultra-modern space-age vehicle of some sort, a Star Wars transport, a least a limousine. Here they are, sitting in a van like a mere mortal.

Anyway, we take about a five-minute ride across the base. Schirra and Carpenter, men in their late '70s, were still lively and animated. At one point in our journey across the base, Wally turns to me and says, "Everything looks a lot different than I am used to. Do you know where we are?"

I just look at him. He is asking me where we are. Here is Wally Schirra, a former U.S. Navy test pilot, the only person to fly in all of America's first three space programs – Mercury, Gemini, and Apollo.

He logged over 295 hours in space. This highly intellectual, accomplished space traveler asked me for directions while driving around in his backyard. At that point, my eyes were so full of stars I couldn't tell him even if I did know. I just shrugged.

Once we got to the outdoor ceremony, I was merely a participant, so I settled among the crowd. The event was a tree-planting ceremony in Cooper's honor at the JSC's Memorial Grove. Next thing I know, I am standing next to one of the former astronauts - Neil Armstrong. The man whose picture was on my wall for all those years is now standing beside me. The nature of the event and wearing the military uniform forced me to maintain my composure. Military bearing is expected from a military chaplain, and the fact that my last name is emblazoned on the right side of my uniform made me easily identifiable!

I tried to soak in the moment. I was standing in a memorial park on a beautiful day in Houston next to an icon from my childhood. Neil and I were just hanging out together! During the ceremony, I kept looking at Armstrong's shoes. They looked like normal feet, but I couldn't help but think that, at one time, they were on the moon.

The third part of the day's events was a gathering with an even smaller number of people to eat cake, finger sandwiches, drinks, etc., at a nearby building. The participants were, again, a few military personnel, NASA representatives, and current and former astronauts. With my glass coffee cup with a little handle on the side, I took the opportunity to visit with a few legends. On the exterior, I was calm, cool, and collected while maintaining my military bearing! I was determined to do this for two reasons. First, drooling on a military uniform is not acceptable for an Air Force officer. Second, I had to fit in. If you looked up the definition of "cool," you would see pictures of these men. They were kind and gracious.

Though far from the Dairy Queen, some of the conversation was the same. Just a group of men gathered to discuss the day's events, their families, and a word or two about the weather.

After a full morning and afternoon, I was taken back to my car. I headed out the gate, my head spinning with a surreal experience to appreciate and remember for the rest of my life.

Seasoned Adults

Some of the sweetest people you will ever meet are senior adults. At the same time, some of the crabbiest people you will ever meet are senior adults. Sometimes they are the same person. Though we all carry a mixture of both, it seems more pronounced in senior adults.

These men and women have stood the test of time. Many have been married. Many have children, grandchildren, and some have great-grandchildren. Some are divorced or widowed. Most have been around the church for a while; some are newcomers to the faith. All are going through similar calamities.

Some popular expressions explain getting old well: everything hurts, and what doesn't hurt doesn't work; the gleam in your eyes is from the sun hitting your bifocals; your little black book contains only names that end in M.D.; your children begin to look middle-aged; the little old gray-haired lady you helped across the street is you wife, you sink your teeth into a steak, and they stay there, you know all the answers, but nobody asks you the questions...and the list goes on.

I have found that senior adults, whom I like to call "seasoned adults, "simply want to feel valued. They know that many things have passed them by. They know that more time is behind them than in front of them. They know their doctor, lawyer, and pastor will all be younger than them! They know this, but they have much to offer.

Some offer their time. They provide ministry to the "shut-ins" and are available for hospital visitation. Craftsmen make things. Mechanics and electricians fix things. Retired teachers teach things. Ladies in the kitchen cook and clean things. One of the jobs of the pastor is to equip members for ministry. A wise minister will tap into the wealth of experience so that they can give their time to minister to the church as a whole. Many offer their prayers. Even those who cannot physically attend church worship and activities can pray for their ministers and for the ministry to flourish.

I have also found that seasoned adults like to have fun! They like to go places and do things together. In fact, it took me a few years to realize how much I had been missing by taking several youth trips and not enough senior adult trips. There are certainly some advantages of leading an overnight seasoned adult trip over being in charge of a youth trip.

Top ten things off the top of my head:

Seasoned adults are fairly self-sufficient. They remember to pack all of their clothes and diligently keep the itinerary intact – in fact, any deviation from the published itinerary will be noted.

- They tend to have very little drama.
- They look out for one another.
- They express their appreciation to the leaders of the trip – sometimes with homemade cookies.
- They rarely yell from the back of the bus, "I'm bored!"
- They like to eat at any opportunity.
- They are generally slower than the pastor.
- They like to go to bed early.
- They have their own rooms.
- Last, and most importantly... they do not sneak out of their rooms at night; if they do, I don't care!

Seasoned adults, like youth, are also spiritually sensitive. They know that life has its endpoint. They have been to enough of their family and friends' funerals to be fully aware of their own mortality. Loving them, understanding them, honoring them, and providing opportunities for them to express their love for the Lord while also giving renewed purpose in the church is the least we can do for these men and women who have paved the way for each of us.

It's Not Always As It Seems

It takes a lot for a preacher to be speechless.

One afternoon, a female church member, Candy, helped Susie clean our house for an upcoming event. They were very industrious, so much so they actually flipped the mattress in our bedroom. When they lifted the mattress, they discovered something a bit eerie. On my side of the bed, between the mattress and the box springs, lay a knife – a large butcher knife.

Though I was not present at the time, Susie said that time stood still as they stared at the knife and then, with wide eyes, stared at each other. With a whisper, Candy asked, "Are you and Randy having problems?!"

Though unspoken, they both may have thought, "What sinister plan did he have in mind?" As the saying goes, "You never know what goes behind closed doors." All sorts of murderous conspiracy theories arose, and I was at the heart of them all.

When I came home, Susie was home alone. I'm sure Candy was preparing her testimony for the inevitable trial. Susie held up the now visible butcher knife and asked, "You care to explain this?" I took her literally and said, "It looks like a large knife."

She replied, "And do you know where I found this?"

I sheepishly replied, "In the drawer?"

"No, under our mattress, on your side!" It was then that time stood still for me. "I didn't put a knife under the mattress...or did I?" My long pause and look of confusion seemed to confirm my guilt.

Though some may have wished for a more sinister explanation, the truth came out after suspicion hung in the air and Susie slept with one eye open. A couple of weeks later, Blake came home from college. When the story was relayed, he admitted he was the guilty culprit.

A couple of months prior, the last time he was home, Susie and I were out of the house. For some reason, he became frightened and slept in our bed, hiding a knife underneath the mattress for protection. He went back to college and forgot about the knife. It could have stayed there for several more months. I mean, let's face it, who flips mattresses?

This misunderstanding reminded me of another event back in Stockdale years prior. Susie was pulling some items from the back of our minivan. She pulled out a maternity top and a pair of shorts – two items that were clearly not hers. Holding them up with crocodile tears forming in her eyes, she asked me, "Whose are these?"

I was caught flat-footed. I had never seen these items of clothes before. I stammered and stuttered so much that guilt was written all over me. I assured her that I had no clue where they came from. I had no explanation, but my ghostly white face was not convincing.

Fortunately, she eventually remembered that one of our church members, one of our very pregnant church members, had left her clothes in the back. This was a fortunate memory on her part as well as mine. If the story had not turned out this way, the hidden knife might have been found on her side of the bed!

Post Office Encounter

Even though I now had a mailbox at the end of my driveway, while in Dickinson, I still went to the Post Office to pick up a package or buy stamps. Like most Post Office visits, it involved waiting in line until you could get to the front counter. One day was particularly slow, and I was particularly in a hurry.

Trying to remain patient and calm (because I am the pastor!), I waited for the line to move. It took me a moment to realize that one of Dickinson's most famous residents was right in front of me. My recognition of him was not as acute because his back was to me, and his clothing was uninspiring. This 70-ish man wore a casual shirt, Bermuda shorts, tennis shoes, and socks pulled up to his calves.

Nevertheless, underneath this casual garb was the legendary Gene Kranz. You may know him as a member of the local Methodist Church. You may know him as a motivational speaker. Though you may not immediately recognize his name, most would remember his flat-top haircut, unique homemade white vest, and leadership in guiding the damaged Apollo 13 spacecraft safely back to Earth.

Gene Kranz, the long-time NASA Flight director, was portrayed by Ed Harris in the 1995 movie; "Apollo 13." He is best remembered for his statement, "Failure is not an option!"

His optimism was infectious. In the middle of the Apollo 13 crisis, he was told by a high-ranking official that this could be the worst disaster NASA had ever faced. He replied, "With all due respect, sir, I believe this will be our finest hour."

As the line weaved, we chatted a bit. Then the line stopped. Though there were three Postal employees, each was dealing with some issue. Everything had ground to a halt. My mind began to wander and wonder, what if Gene suddenly took charge of the situation? I could hear him ask, "Is this an instrumentation problem, or are we looking at a real power loss here?" And, "O.K., lets everybody keep cool... let's work the problem, people, let's not make things worse by guessing!" "I don't care about what anything was <u>designed</u> to do. I care about what it <u>can</u> do."

In my thoughts, with a crescendo, he would add, "If we work the problem, today in this Post Office could be our finest hour!" With deafening applause from my fellow line members, he would look with his steely eyes and proclaim, "Failure is not an option!"

When the line took another step forward, my temporary vision was interrupted. Nothing much had changed. Instead, disappointedly, Gene waited patiently like everybody else until he was eventually called to come to the front counter.

Two thoughts come to mind. First, every great hero also wears Bermuda shorts (or those like them) and puts them on one leg at a time. The greats must wait in line. They must occasionally ride in vans. They get colds and headaches. Sometimes they forget things. Sometimes they need a nap. Though we like to put our heroes on a pedestal, they are men and women like us. Though they may have achieved some incredible accomplishments, they have the same basic physical, emotional, mental, and spiritual needs as anyone else.

Second, history hinges on ordinary people like Gene Kranz, who can stare down a challenge despite the odds and mobilize a group of people around a common cause to bring about extraordinary results. Spiritually, may we never shy away from a challenge that is well within the aperture of God's vision. Let us always be willing to be ordinary people ready to do extraordinary things through the supernatural power of our God. Let us also be determined to be at the front of the charge and not be the grumbler in the rear.

You may feel as if the church is not able to meet the challenges of the day. You may feel that the future is bleak. You may feel that we should give up. With all due respect, I believe that we are in our finest hour! The victory is already won. Yes, there are challenges and giants in the land, but God whispers in our ears, "Be strong and courageous, do not be fearful, do not be dismayed, for the Lord your God will be with you wherever you go." Let's live it, people! Lives are hanging in the balance!

On Mission

The Great Commission, given by Jesus, is found in Matthew 28:19-20: "Go therefore and teach all nations, baptizing them in the name of the Father, and of the Son, and of the Holy Spirit, teaching them to observe all things whatsoever I have commanded you and lo, I am with you always, even to the end of the earth." We also read in Acts 1:8, where Jesus says, "But you will receive power when the Holy Spirit comes on you; and you will be my witnesses in Jerusalem, in all Judea and Samaria, and to the ends of the earth." The church has a mission to spread the Good News of Christ – moving from the church's local neighborhood to the ends of the earth.

FBC Dickinson embraced the mission mandate. They were actively involved in the community in various capacities, carrying with them the message of the Gospel. Along with the weekly ministries were specialized, focused ministries to reach the community. A massive Fall Festival in the church gym and an enormous Easter Egg Hunt at a local elementary school introduced families to the church and pointed them to Jesus. Youth Retreats, Youth Camps, Children Camps, and Vacation Bible School planted seeds of the Gospel. Like Yorktown and Stockdale, FBC Dickinson also gave to the Southern Baptist Cooperative Program – enabling churches of all sizes to give to multiple local, national, and international ministries.

One of the highlights of our summer program was the annual mission trip. A group of adults and youth would spend a week at a designated spot – sometimes as close as a struggling church in Galveston, sometimes to hurricane-ravaged East Texas, and sometimes to an impoverished area of Mexico. I enjoyed the trips for several reasons.

Foremost, I was amazed that a group of people – both young and old - could be so dedicated to work in hot, humid, dusty, and stinking conditions with no pay and then enjoy it so much! One area we ministered was just outside of Matamoras, Mexico, across from the U.S. city of Harlingen. We provided a day-long mini vacation Bible School and Worship to a group of children who attended the church named "Dios Provera" or "God will Provide." The name was fitting because these children were the offspring of men and women who worked at the city dump. The church and surrounding simple homes were located at the city dump.

Mission trips like this change the lives of young Americans who witness such austere conditions. Mission trips are also educating. Allow me to share two. The first is shared at my expense. Back home in Dickinson, in the months preceding the Mexico trip, I made regular announcements during the morning worship (unconsciously), showing off my knowledge of Spanish (which is just above zero). I would mention the name of the church, "Dios Provera." I even made a special point to roll the "r" in "Provera." I learned this technique from other Spanish speakers. I never took a formal Spanish course. In high school, I elected to take German over Spanish. This was a critical misstep for a young man living in South Texas.

I was somewhat pleased with my ability to roll my r with such proficiency. It wasn't until late in the summer when one of our church members, a Hispanic who spoke fluent Spanish, asked me, "Pastor, what are you trying to say?" Surprised that he didn't know basic Spanish, I proudly said, "Dios Provera (with the accent on the "e"), you know, "God will provide." He gently said, "You mean "Provera (with the accent on the "a"). He then informed me Provera (with the accent on the "e") is the name of a Mexican contraceptive! I looked stunned. I mentally wrote the first of at least two mission trip lessons – know what you are talking about, and better yet, stick with the language you know!

The second lesson I learned was on this same trip, across the river from Matamoras to the US side of Harlingen. The adults and youth also led a Bible School and the children in Worship at this Spanish-speaking church. In addition, during the afternoon, the youth and adults spruced up, painted, and decorated each Sunday School room. It topped off a great week, and we were proud of the new look.

The following year, the mission group from Dickinson returned to the area. I met with the pastor and took a look around the church building. To my surprise, much of our work had been changed – new colors on the walls, new pictures, etc.

At first, I was offended, and then I was a bit ashamed. I realized that our group, though well-meaning, had descended into their space and changed it. What seems obvious now, instead of putting our Anglo, Houston-area church look on their walls, we should have partnered with the members of the Harlingen church that ministered in the room. They would have had their own thoughts. They would have had their own opinions. Another lesson learned: partnership is a two-way street. May we never be so presumptuous that we think our way of doing things is the gold standard.

Even after all these years of ministry, lessons will always be learned.

Pets

I have had pets most of my married life. When Susie and I were dating, she asked me if I liked cats. Since I grew up with cats in my house, I said, "Yes." Little did I know that I checked off one of the requirements of a future spouse! As a newly married couple, our first pet was a calico cat. We named her "Josie," the cat of many colors. I was in Seminary and had to have a name with Biblical connotations.

As mentioned, in Yorktown, we had a cat named "Max" and added a dog named "Licky." In Stockdale, we had an assortment of animals – dogs, cats, rabbits, gerbils, hamsters, hermit crabs, and a goldfish. We never named the goldfish, but if we did, it would have been "Lazarus." That goldfish came in a see-through plastic bag. I don't remember, but it probably came from the Watermelon Jubilee.

We placed it in a cheap, small fishbowl. Everybody knows that fish in this environment do not live long – except for Lazarus. The bowl had to be cleaned regularly. Sometimes we would forget, and Lazarus had to swim in the murky water. One memorable day, Susie cleaned the bowl. The fish was transferred to a smaller water-filled container. As Susie cleaned the bowl, she realized the temperature in the room was cool and thought a little warm water would be nice for the fish. She didn't realize that the water she placed in the bowl was much too warm, perhaps scalding.

When she transferred Lazarus to the bigger steaming hot bowl of water, the fish had only one recourse – jump! It was in a quandary because fish need water to live, and this steamy bowl was the only source available. So, like a miniature Sea World act, this goldfish jumped up for relief from the heat and then back down to breathe. This took place in a matter of seconds until the fish was retrieved and rescued. Lazarus lived many more months until he finally died and was flushed to a watery grave. At least, I think that is what happened. 300-pound Lazarus may be enjoying a Caribbean vacation recounting the time he was almost boiled alive!

In Dickinson, we had a dog named Elsie. Elsie was a Boston Terrier with unusual markings. She had white fur on her face. Her eyes, instead of the traditional brown, were light blue. She was, well, unique. When she rode in the car with us, she would sit on the front seat and look out the window. People would turn and point. One of Amanda's friends asked, "What is that?" She sheepishly replied, "That's my dog."

She not only scared humans, but she also scared other dogs. Once, a neighbor's dog was chasing Elsie from behind. When Elsie looked at the chasing dog, the aggressor looked terrified, turned, and ran away.

Elsie also had a bladder problem. It was triggered by a pat on the stomach. When a visitor came to the house, Elsie immediately turned over on her back. We would have to yell across the house, "Don't touch her!" Our guests thought that she was ferocious and would trigger some violent reactions. They were partly true. The violent reaction was a massive release by her bladder!

One day, Elsie broke her leg. I will not go into the details of how she broke her leg – you will need to talk with Susie and the actions of her husband and son. It was a bad enough break; the leg had to be set, and poor Elsie had a little pink cast on her front leg. One day, she got out of the house and was nowhere to be found. I got in the car to search the neighborhood. I spotted her (she was the only strange-looking dog with a pink cast) and drove to her. She compliantly got in the car. I said to her, "Elsie, what is wrong with you? Why do you run off? Where did you think you were going? We feed you; we protect you; what is so great about running away – especially with a cast on your leg." She just looked at me with her scrunched face and blue eyes.

On the drive back, I couldn't help but think about Jesus comparing us to sheep – sheep who have gone astray. It doesn't make sense that we would stray and run from the One who gives us everything. Despite my lack of trust and disobedience, I am grateful that, as we read in Psalm 23, the Good Shepherd "restores my soul and leads me in paths of righteousness."

Aren't You My Neighbor?

Visitors would come to our church on Sunday mornings. In an attempt to show our friendliness, we would greet them at the door, give them a church bulletin and help them find a seat. Once seated, they would peruse the bulletin and hopefully notice the perforated section that would invite them to fill out the information and place it in the offering plate when it is passed later in the service (those last 19 words were regularly voiced during the announcement time.) These perforated parts of the bulletin would then be given to me the next day.

Like a well-oiled machine, a group of women would bake a small loaf of bread, and one of our deacons delivered the bread following the Wednesday evening service. The hope is that they would appreciate the effort, realize how friendly and thoughtful we were, and maybe as a bonus, realize that Jesus is the bread of life (OK, maybe that was a stretch!) Most were appreciative. One couple commented at the door of their home, "This is great, thanks! This will go great with the jam Bay Area Baptist gave us last week!"

One Wednesday, I noted that the visitor card indicated that the couple was my neighbor who lived in the street directly behind me. I told the bread delivery deacon I could take this one and deliver it on my way home. So, I drove to my neighborhood. Through the darkness, I saw the correct address and walked up to the door with bread in hand. I was a bit surprised, knowing that the couple was elderly, that they lived in such a big two-story home.

I rang the doorbell, and a younger man opened the door. Looking at the card, I asked if Mr. and Mrs (calling them by name) were home. He looked somewhat bewildered and said they didn't live there. He then pointed across the street about three houses down and asked, "Don't you live there?" I looked, and sure enough, there was my house. I was on the wrong street.

I apologized for my mistake and felt guilty for not knowing my neighbor. I drove one street over and then completed my bread delivery. In the following weeks, I kept my eye on the big two-story home three doors down and across the street from my house. I hardly ever saw the young man outside, but as fate would have it, I tripped on my water hose one day when walking down my sidewalk. After catching my balance, my first instinct was to look toward the end of the street, and sure enough, there he was in his yard, giving a pathetic shake of the head. My humanity was again on full display.

Looking for Randy Marshall

"Can I speak to Randy Marshall?"

Upon hearing the question on our home phone, Susie answered, "He's not here right now. Can I leave a message?

Pause.

"Who is this?" asked the man on the other end of the line.

Susie replies, "This is his wife."

Pause.

He answers, "I definitely have the wrong number!"

This interaction was the first time we realized there were (at least) two Randy Marshalls in the Galveston County area. One was the pastor of the First Baptist Church in Dickinson. The second was the leader of a honky-tonk band named "Randy Marshall and the Law." Apparently, the second Randy Marshall did not have a wife.

Though some may see some similarities in our two vocations, for the most part, they were worlds apart. We received a couple of more calls looking for the single Randy Marshall. On one occasion, I answered the phone. The person asked for Randy Marshall. I said, "This is Randy."

The voice on the other end was looking for a band to play at his event. He gave me the date and asked if I was available. A quick mental note of my calendar revealed that on this particular Saturday, I was available. It was very tempting to agree to come and bring my "act." I thought about taking along our Youth Minister, who led a Youth Praise Band on Wednesday, and preaching a sermon to the crowd. Though it was tempting and would have been extremely fun, I finally admitted to the caller that he had reached the wrong Randy Marshall.

Years later, I learned that a young, brash evangelist named Billy Graham had faced a similar situation. In 1946, Billy Graham and a youth ministry team were en-route to England on an evangelistic tour. They became stranded by weather overnight at a Newfoundland air force base. The base's social director gave the rag-tag team a once-over and concluded they were a vaudeville act.

Graham and his team were asked to perform. Ever eager for an opportunity to preach the gospel, Graham and the team accepted the invitation to entertain the troops. When the base commander realized their true purpose a few minutes into their "act," he flew into a rage and threatened to lock them up. I might have accepted the invitation if I had read this account sooner. At least I could say that Billy Graham and I both performed similar acts in an unconventional setting!

24-Hour Silent Retreat

One educational goal I had desired over the years was a Doctor of Ministry Degree (DMin.) I learned about an opportunity just up the road in Houston. The Houston Graduate School of Theology was offering a degree program specifically for military chaplains. This was an interesting degree program for a school that had roots in the Quaker tradition – one that practiced pacifism.

In 2006, this evangelical school was broadening its influence and offering this degree. Like most doctoral programs, it was small – eight of us from varying denominational backgrounds and military chaplaincies. The program consisted of intense week-long workshops on campus followed by weeks of at-home reading and writing assignments.

One of the activities during this program was participating in an overnight retreat at a Roman Catholic Retreat Center. This was unlike any retreat I had ever been – it was a 24-hour silent retreat. The retreat center consisted of a large sanctuary, various meeting rooms, and an expansive outdoor campus. Though serene, it was located in the heart of Houston. Our assignment was to get alone with God and listen to His voice. Though I would see others and gesture to them, no talking was permitted. During the day and evening, I could go to my small, single, dorm-style room, with no T.V., to contemplate even more.

Randy Marshall

I will say the first couple of hours were great. I was away from the pressures and load of the church. At the time, my heart was heavy from family pressures – I missed Blake, who had graduated and gone to Texas A&M. I was concerned for some of the pressures that Amanda was facing, I was concerned for Susie's health, and I was intensely burdened over my sister, Sandy who was at MD Anderson undergoing cancer treatments. Here, in this retreat, I was able to focus on my spiritual life, a sort of spiritual cleansing from the world. What began as a welcome exercise became difficult. I was a doer, and I wasn't doing anything!

As my spirit calmed, I saw and heard nature more acutely. I picked up on distant sounds. I took the time to read God's Word, not to work on a sermon but to allow His Word to speak to me truly. The 24 hours came and went. I survived and learned a few things.

On a related note, I had volunteered to drive a couple of my fellow students back to the campus after our experience. I drove out of the retreat center, down a narrow road, to a larger road, to the access ramp onto I-45. As I was entering the ramp, some great Houstonian cut me off. I immediately slammed the brakes to avoid an accident. As he crossed in front of me, he put up a finger. He may have been saying that I was number one, but I am not sure.

I realized at that point that lessons learned in the silent retreat were put to the test. Though it wasn't intended to be part of the curriculum, it was a reminder that life is not lived in solitude and peace. The world we live in is fast-paced, aggressive, and sometimes deadly. The key to our faith is to take that inner peace that Christ provides, a peace that passes all understanding, and apply it to our sometimes-crazy world. Our peace is not confined to a space or an experience. His peace follows us because He is our peace. Yes, we can have peace in our hearts even when the world is whirling around us!

Jingling of the Keys

As in Yorktown and Stockdale, Dickinson had a mid-week service in the Fellowship Hall. In Dickinson, multiple groups were meeting at the same time. The youth were in the Fellowship Hall. Children met in the children's area, and adults met in the Fellowship Hall. For the adults, Wednesday night included a time of prayer and devotion.

Some observations of this time of prayer. Please understand, before I share, I believe in the power of prayer. Corporately and privately, prayer should always be a priority in the church and the lives of believers. Of all the visible outward actions of Jesus upon the earth, including preaching, teaching, and healing – it was prayer that the disciples asked to learn. "Lord, teach us to pray!"

In reading Jesus' prayers and the prayers throughout Scripture, we quickly see that our prayers pale in comparison. Instead of the lofty words lifted to our Lord that address the redemptive purposes of our lives and highlight the kingdom of God, many times, we have relegated our prayers to a list of known physical needs – cardiac issues, broken bones, upcoming surgeries, stubbed toes, skinned knees, etc.

All these things should be in our thoughts and prayers, but we should not stop there! Praying for our nation and community, praying for eyes to be open to the Gospel message, praying for ongoing outreach opportunities, and more. These should be highlighted as well! Though our prayers should focus on the majesty and holiness of God, the one praying the prayer should be humble and contrite without using words meant to impress. Prayers should be genuine. I love the prayers of children when they come to Christ, which sound something like, "God, this is John; I'm sorry for the bad things I have done. I love you." Now that is a prayer!

Another reminder, God is omniscient – he is all-knowing. He does not need a roadmap to be informed of the needs of His people. For example, I have heard people pray like this, "Dear Lord, we also need to pray for Bob Smith; he is at Clear Lake Hospital, room 210, and is scheduled for a quadruple bypass and would appreciate our prayers..."

Many times, this type of prayer is given when the one praying forgets to mention the request before the prayer begins. I always imagine God hearing this prayer and acting surprised – as if He is the first to hear about this! I could go on. Suffice it to say God hears our prayers, as imperfect as they may be. I would imagine that the angels snicker a bit at our fumbling and stumbling around the throne room of God!

Again, like Yorktown and Stockdale, the regular Wednesday night schedule was adjusted once a month for the monthly church conference. These church conferences or business meetings focused on the church budget and expenditures. It also featured upcoming ministries and programs and, at times, concerns/comments about ministries, programs, and their budgetary requirements. These meetings tended to take longer than necessary.

One of our dear ladies had a system to inform me when she was done. It was a multi-step process. When she felt the meeting should be wrapping up, her first step was reaching under her chair and placing her purse on the table where she sat. As the meeting continued, she would put her purse on her lap. Next, she would then open the purse, grab her car keys, and hold them. Finally, when her meeting quotient had been met, she would gently jingle the keys, a sign that the meeting was now over for her. It was time to go home. I don't remember her ever leaving the room if the meeting went past the jingling of the keys. However, I am certain that words spoken beyond that point, for her, were unintelligible.

Like the game of baseball, church has no time limit, and at times, both extend into extra innings. Whereas extra innings, sudden death, or overtime is exciting for the sports fan, it is rarely met with the same enthusiasm by the average church member. Whether it is a church service or a business conference, an extended period of time can be counterproductive. As the saying goes, "The mind can absorb what the seat can endure!"

From my average church readers, I can almost hear an audible "amen!"

Influence

Reflecting on the first 22 years of pastoral ministry – from Yorktown to Stockdale to Dickinson, I have had the opportunity to lead, share, and interact with men and women of faith. Our relationship is not only pastor to church member but also friend to friend.

Their lives toward me, the body of Christ, and the world they live in have been incredibly impactful. Unfortunately, our churches see vocational ministers as superstars of faithfulness. Sure, vocational ministers have been called, set apart, trained, and gained vast ministerial experience. Many have given up much to be called "pastor" or "minister." But, never let us elevate a vocational minister over the importance of those in everyday jobs and positions, including those in our homes.

Scripture is full of ordinary men and women who made a difference – farmers, shepherds, hunters, coppersmiths, goldsmiths, silversmiths, merchants, potters, masons, singers, musicians, businessmen and women, tentmakers, soldiers, armor-bearers, jailers, carpenters, fishermen; the list goes on. Some were in high positions of authority – kings, queens, governors, Magi from the East, doctors, tax collectors, and teachers of the law.

As a pastor, some of the most impressive men and women of faith I have met have been doctors, lawyers, bankers, teachers, military members, administrators, construction workers, plant workers, mailmen, salespeople; the list goes on. Let us always remember the unsung and often overlooked vocation of "homemaker." These men and women have been part of the fabric of faith throughout history.

Scripturally, as believers, they are "saints." They are "ministers." As I often relay to congregations, "There are some people I will never be able to impact as much as you." Pastors and other ministers are expected to be interested in the church and God. Personal conversation and action become more noticeable when an everyday person speaks and lives for Christ.

In Dickinson, I think of one person who went the extra mile. Cliff Farmer was an engineer at NASA working with robotics. This longtime employee was a supervisor and was in the higher echelon of NASA. But you wouldn't know it.

At the church, Cliff was the low-key, deep-thinking young deacon. Cliff was the high-school youth Sunday School teacher. Cliff was the one setting up chairs for the next event. Cliff was the youth camp counselor. Cliff was an integral part of mission trips, including several trips to the city dump. Cliff played in the Wednesday evening youth praise band. Cliff was on the Pastoral Search committee when we were called to Dickinson and always had a keen interest in my family – Susie, Blake, and Amanda. My children and a host of others under his and his wife Kari's guidance will tell you that his life, demeanor, and actions changed their lives.

I am saddened to say that Cliff recently died after a long bout with cancer. His life touched others. He joins others in my memory who were willing to stand for truth, speak the truth, and go the extra mile to advance the Kingdom of God. To them, both living and dead, I give a humble "thanks!"

The Message

The journey of being a local pastor in my three pastorates was extremely rewarding. I have always felt privileged to share the truth of the Word of God and help others in their spiritual journey. It has been my greatest privilege. I have learned much about the church, its members, and myself in 22 years. My perspective as a 47-year-old was a bit different from my 25-year-old former self. One thing that never changed was the age-old, transformational message of the Gospel.

2008 marked the 50th anniversary of NASA. In celebration of its 50th anniversary, NASA beamed the Beatle's song, "Across the Universe," into deep space. On February 4, 2008, NASA's Deep Space Network transmitted the tune from Madrid Spain, and aimed it for the star Polaris – the North Star. Even though it travels across the universe at a speed of 186,000 miles a second, it will take 431 years along a long and winding road to reach its final destination – 2.5 quadrillion miles away!

Former Beatle Paul McCartney expressed excitement over this – he sent a message saying, "Amazing, Well done, NASA! Send my love to the aliens. All the best, Paul."

We marvel that we live in a time when digital messages can be sent, skipping across the universe to unknown recipients. When we take a step back, however, we realize that as believers, we are entrusted with a message that is even more miraculous.

There is another kind of message that has already been sent and received across an even greater expanse. These words, though, have not been sent digitally through the unknowns of deep space. The most powerful words transmitted across the universe come not from Earth to space but from the glories of heaven to the hearts of men and women. They are given personally, intimately, and sacrificially by the creator of the universe Himself. This message of salvation is not limited to an era of time or a select group of people. The Easter phrase, "He is Risen," reverberates through the ages and provides hope for all.

The apostle Paul provides a spiritual insight in Philippians 2:6-11 as he describes the wonders of the message of Jesus, the One who is "the name above all names." You may also want to reread the accounts of the death, burial, and resurrection of Jesus found in Matthew 26-28, Mark 14-16, Luke 22-24, and John 17-20. These words of life have been personally delivered from across the universe. Read, accept, live, and wonder in them as the Giver of these penetrates your heart and transforms your life!

Farewell

After serving as a local church pastor for 22 years and as a part-time Reserve Air Force Chaplain for almost 20 years, I was given an opportunity to serve in the full-time military. In many ways, the opportunity was a once-in-a-lifetime offer for a Reserve Air Force Chaplain. I was at a point of decision. After much prayer, consideration, and continual conversations with Susie, I accepted.

Saying "yes" came with some risks. Not only would we uproot and move to Doral, Fl, in the Miami area, but the opportunity was limited to three years. There were no full-time military guarantees after this three-year tour. We said "yes," because I sensed the calling of God. Military Chaplains are given a unique opportunity to speak to our men and women in uniform and speak words of truth in this institutional setting. The new calling also invigorated me to face a new challenge in a new place.

Below are words written to FBC Dickinson when I left.

Ten years.

Ten years ago, back in 1998, members of the First Baptist Church, Dickinson, began referring to me as "my pastor." Susie, twelve-year-old Blake, and eleven-year-old Amanda and I picked up our belongings from tiny Stockdale, Texas, and moved to the town of Dickinson. A partnership was formed as together, we faced the joys and sorrows, challenges and victories, and the good and bad of everyday life.

On a national level, we saw the election and reelection of a new president. We witnessed the horrors of airplanes slamming into tall buildings. We prayed for the troops heading off to fight a new kind of war. We witnessed fluctuations in the economy and a shaky housing market. We grieved over those facing Tsunamis. We were able to shine in helping our Louisiana neighbors find food and shelter after a devastating hurricane. Then, just like that, we were the ones evacuating, facing an uncertain future while being stuck in a seemingly endless quagmire of traffic. Looking back, we have a lot of stories to tell.

I have had the opportunity to share in the joy of a wedding celebration as well as grieve with you in the midst of a funeral service. We have prayed together, played together, worshipped together, ministered together, laughed, and cried together. Some of you were there in the beginning. Others have come along the way. It truly is humbling to know that for some of our children, I am the only pastor they have ever known. Ten years have passed. My kids are older, my hair is grayer, my bones are creakier, but all in all, my life is fuller. Thank you for ten years of telling others, "This is my pastor."

Thank you for your support and prayers even when I was not at my best. Thank you for a decade of allowing me to shepherd you as together we sought to be the salt of the earth and the light of the world. Ten years have passed, and if God allows, we will have more stories to tell in the coming days. Let's together seek Him as He reveals His will and way in 2008 and beyond.

Pastor Randy

Epilogue

"Jesus did many other things as well. If every one of them were written down, I suppose that even the whole world would not have room for the books that would be written."
John 21:25

These closing words were written by the Apostle John in the Gospel that bears his name. The point that John writes is that more, much more could have been written. While, obviously, I am not comparing my writing to the book of John, I understand this sentiment. In reviewing a twenty-two-year span in my life, much more could have been written! Some of these things involve trivial moments (even more trivial) that could have been shared. I could have included additional highs and lows of family life and ministry. Some memories would require a conversation around the kitchen table with a cup of coffee in hand. I am also aware of the acronym "TLDR," meaning "too long, didn't read!" I heard the keys jingling and decided this was a good place to stop!

So, in 2008, a chapter of our lives ended, but another was about to begin with others to follow. As I stated in the introduction, my purpose in writing this book is three-fold – first, to provide a behind-the-scenes glimpse into the life of one minister and his family. Second, to provide some honest perspective and insight so that church members could greater appreciate their pastor's spirituality and humanity. And third, to encourage the reader to reflect upon their own stories and share them with family and friends. Hopefully, reading this book brought some perspective, insight, inspiration, and an occasional smile.

It is true, "Sometimes you will never know the value of a moment until it becomes a memory." I pray you keep your eyes and ears open, valuing the moments and treasuring the precious memories.

In 2008, the Marshalls faced a new challenge and a huge transition. We were about to embark on a new journey, a full-time adventure with the United States Air Force. "The Marshall Chronicles: Aim High Edition" was about to begin!

www.ingramcontent.com/pod-product-compliance
Lightning Source LLC
Chambersburg PA
CBHW060511090426
42735CB00011B/2182